CHARLES CHURCHILL
SELECTED POETRY

CHARLES CHURCHILL
SELECTED POETRY

Edited with an introduction by Adam Rounce

TRENT EDITIONS

Published by Trent Editions 2003

Trent Editions
Department of English and Media Studies
The Nottingham Trent University
Clifton Lane.
Nottingham NG11 8NS

This edition © Trent Books
Introduction © Adam Rounce

All rights reserved. No part of this book may be
reproduced in any form except by a newspaper or
magazine reviewer who wishes to quote brief
passages in connection with a review.

Printed in Great Britain by Goaters Limited, Nottingham

ISBN 1 84233 096 9

Contents

Acknowledgements	VI
Introduction	VII
Further Reading	XXXII
Selected Poems	
[From *The Rosciad*]	1
[From *The Ghost*]	4
The Prophecy of Famine: a Scots Pastoral	13
An Epistle to William Hogarth	32
[From *The Duellist*]	53
[From *Gotham*]	57
The Farewell	65
The 'Dedication to the Sermons'	82
Notes	88
Index of titles and first lines	122

Acknowledgements

This edition would not have been possible without the support of a Special Research Fellowship from the Leverhulme Trust. I would also like to thank those who have had to read a great amount of either Churchill or my writings on him, namely Tom Mason, David Hopkins, David Fairer and Andrew Bennett. Other people who have helped with my Churchillian work (sometimes unwittingly) include Nick Groom, Abigail Williams, Paddy Bullard, Conrad Brunstrom, Hamish Mathison, Robert Jones, Dafydd Moore, Brian Young, Ben Hawes and Eleanor Pridgeon. At the University of Bristol the librarians in the Special Collections of the Arts and Social Sciences Library, along with the secretarial staff of the Department of English, also deserve my gratitude. Finally, I owe a great deal to John Goodridge and John Lucas, for years of encouragement.

Introduction

'The Glory and the Nothing of a Name'

In 1816, half a century after the death of Charles Churchill (1731-64), Byron penned 'Churchill's Grave', a comment on the ephemeral nature of poetic celebrity. Churchill's grave at Dover had already become an obscure spot, visited sporadically by the odd literary type showing their respects to a figure from another age. Byron records the 'natural homily' of the Sexton, who when asked about the grave, believes that its occupant 'Was a most famous writer in his day'. This, for Byron, encapsulates 'Obscurity and Fame / The Glory and the Nothing of a Name'. The poem is a meditation on Byron's own ideas of the ultimate shallowness of public notability and the arbitrary fate of everyone in the light of posterity. Yet it is no coincidence that he alights upon a figure sympathetic to his own aesthetic: a satirist immensely popular in his own time, famous for the savagery of his attacks upon an inept and mendacious government, corrupt placemen, vain literary celebrities, hypocritical churchmen, and facile intellectuals. In Churchill, Byron selected the most cohesive, sustained and successful English poetic satirist between the death of his beloved Alexander Pope in 1744, and his own emergence in the 1800s.

For the full weight of its message to come across, Byron's poem takes Churchill's former success to be as great as his present obscurity. Indeed, not the least remarkable side of Churchill's story is his meteoric rise to poetic fame and fortune. His first published poem, *The Rosciad* (1761) was an enormous success, running to eight editions within two years. Thirteen other satires and two significant fragmentary works were also produced by the time of his death three years later, in November 1764. All were successful, with many quickly running to new editions. It has been

INTRODUCTION

estimated that Churchill earned at least £3,500 from his poetry, a huge sum for the times.[1] From being a poor and obscure clergyman, Churchill became rich, famous and feared. Yet, by the end of the century, when the topicality of its issues had worn away, the very particularity of Churchill's vigorous satire could easily seem remote, obscure and far from relevant. His reputation suffered even further as the nineteenth century progressed. To trace Churchill's peculiar journey from obscurity to fame and back to obscurity again, we need to look briefly at his life before and then during the immersion in contemporary politics which was to change his career utterly.

Life and Times

Charles Churchill was born in Westminster in February 1731. His father, also called Charles, was the curate of St John the Evangelist, Westminster, and the vicar of Rainham in Kent. All we know of the poet's mother is a hint in the poetry that she was Scottish.[2] Churchill was admitted to Westminster school in 1741 (his fellows at Westminster including Bonnell Thornton, George Colman, Robert Lloyd and William Cowper). He then went to St John's, Cambridge, in 1748 (a college associated with Westminster), yet never matriculated, and does not seemed to have stayed at College long, whether due to financial problems or other reasons.[3] He secretly married Martha Scott (in what was then known as a 'Fleet marriage', since it was performed clandestinely by one of the parsons of the Fleet Prison) around 1749. Churchill's father, apparently a lenient man, supported the young couple; Churchill was still intended for the Church, and although he and his wife went to Sunderland for a time, they were back in London by 1754, when he was ordained a deacon. His first posting was to the curacy of South Cadbury and Sparkford in Somerset.[4] Two years later, Churchill was ordained a priest, and this promotion led him to become curate of Rainham in Kent, his father's parish, for the next two years. The incomes of minor clergyman in this period were meagre, to say the least, and it seems Churchill attempted to supplement his income by running a school in Rainham, and by teaching in London.[5] In 1758, the death of his father meant that he took up the curacy of St John's in Westminster. This alleviated his financial problems somewhat, but he was still badly off; in 1760, he was saved from debtors' prison only through the help of Pierson Lloyd (Under-Master at Westminster school and the father of his friend, Robert), who arranged a settlement with his creditors.

Some of Churchill's early poetic attempts have survived. His friendship with Lloyd and George Colman (who had recently satirised the fashionable Pindaric odes of Thomas Gray, in their odes 'to Obscurity' and 'to Oblivion' of 1760), produced some fragmentary squibs and satires. He appears to have taken up his pen more concertedly principally to make money. His first published poem, *The Rosciad*, a satire on contemporary actors, came out in March 1761; unable to find a publisher willing to risk money on it, Churchill funded it himself (a shrewd financial decision as it turned out, since he benefited directly from its immediate success and its seven reprints). The subject of the poem was far from novel: eighteenth-century theatre was the most popular source of gossip, scandal and unconfined opinion on the merits or otherwise of performers (the level of hostility towards a bad play would shock a genteel modern audience). Churchill, having viewed the foibles, follies and vanities of actors at close hand, utilised the voyeuristic appeal of these celebrities, and produced a poem that, like Pope's *Dunciad*, gained a readership through its universal attraction. After all, everyone had an opinion on the subjects of its satire (including the subjects themselves).

The success of *The Rosciad* produced a sequel. *The Apology*, addressed to the *Critical Reviewers* (May 1761) was motivated partly by a notice in the *Critical Review*, which claimed that *The Rosciad* was the work of Bonnell Thornton, Robert Lloyd or George Colman. Churchill suspected the review to have been written by the editor, the novelist Tobias Smollett, who would soon become Churchill's enemy for political reasons. This attack on the morals and motives of literary criticism was followed by *Night* (November 1761), in which the poet addresses his friend Robert Lloyd. The poem is an apologia for Churchill's bohemian lifestyle and worldview, castigating the hypocritical mores of the supposedly prudent who pretend to upright morals..

It is clear that fame and relative fortune had changed Churchill; the impoverished clergyman was now something of a dandy about town. Rumours of his loose living proliferated, and it appears that he separated from his wife around this time.[6] He even, in a tangential way, seems to have been involved with the so-called 'Hell Fire Club', otherwise known as the Monks of Medenham Abbey. This notorious gathering of dissolute figures, organised amongst others by two more of Churchill's future enemies, the Earl of Sandwich and Sir Francis Dashwood, also included the man who was to have the most influence on the remainder of Churchill's public and poetic career – John Wilkes.

'The Northern Machiavel'

From an historical distance it is sometimes hard to understand how John Wilkes (1727-97), a relatively humble MP, became the most lionised and infamous politician of his time. The story, as far at least as Churchill's involvement goes, properly begins in 1761, and the debates on ending the Seven Years War. Since 1756, the War had been organised with considerable success by William Pitt the Elder (1708-78). However, the accession of the new King, George III, in 1760, changed the political landscape considerably, mainly by encouraging the rise of his former tutor, John Stuart, third Earl of Bute (1713-92), a man destined to become the butt of much of Churchill's satire. In October 1761, Pitt resigned as Secretary of State, because of his failure to get the King and Privy Council to declare war on Spain (a country thought to be plotting with the ostensible enemy, France). Pitt's brother-in-law, Earl Temple, was a patron to Wilkes, and he and Churchill would support the views of Pitt throughout the next three controversial years. In effect, this meant opposing Bute's increasingly powerful administration in almost every matter, though the (popular) Pittite call for the continuation of the war until sufficiently harsh terms could be imposed on France was the beginning and the centre of the argument.

After Pitt's resignation, and that of the Duke of Newcastle in May

INTRODUCTION

1762, the Earl of Bute became First Lord of the Treasury and therefore, effectively, Prime Minister. Although Bute has been treated more favourably by modern historians, he was vilified and attacked by his contemporaries to an extent that seems extraordinary today: on at least two occasions, he was lucky not to have been torn apart by an angry crowd. There are a number of reasons for his astonishing unpopularity. He was following the momentum of Pitt's successful pursuit of the War, a pursuit he seemed to want to reverse. He was not a career politician so much as a courtier, and the King's friendship did him no favours in the eyes of his contemporaries, who saw Bute as an inept product of nepotism; certainly Bute's urbane and refined background did little to prepare him for the ferocity of political life. Furthermore, and perhaps most importantly, he was Scottish.

It is difficult to overestimate the degree of anti-Scottish feeling in England in the early 1760s. According to John Brewer, 'the Scots, especially in London, enjoyed the dubious distinction of being even more unpopular than the Jews'.[7] Herbert Atherton, in an analysis of the print satires aimed at Bute, agrees: 'Anti-Scottish prejudice was as much a part of the nativism of the middling and lower classes as was hatred of the French'.[8] The reasons for this prejudice were various: the Act of Union of 1707 had been followed by the failed Jacobite risings of 1715 and 1745, both of which were exploited repeatedly as examples of Scottish perfidy and treachery. The Scots were supposedly penurious, miserly, selfish and cunning; and in a sad prefiguring of more modern rhetoric on immigration, the movement of Scots to seek their fortune in London (and the success of Scottish artists, writers and thinkers there) was seen as only the beginning of the supposed 'swamping' of England. Other descriptions of the time, both verbal and pictorial, repeatedly describe the Scots as a starving, disease-ridden people, scratching at their lice and scabies. The well-known prejudices of Samuel Johnson towards the Scots in this period seem almost benign (and even parodic) when compared to the ferocious insults that formed a staple of the writings and prints of his contemporaries.

Latent anti-Scots prejudice after the failed Jacobite rebellion of Charles

INTRODUCTION

Edward Stuart ('Bonnie Prince Charlie') in 1745 was revived by Bute's accession to power. In many ways, he was a godsend to any political satirist. He was seen as the favourite of a young king ('the favourite' was the most popular of the many insulting sobriquets attached to Bute, although 'the Northern Machiavel' suggests the intolerance of the times very well). Consequently he could be accused of despotically abusing his country through his control of a pliant monarch. Scurrilous rumours made him the lover of Augusta, the Dowager Princess of Wales; historical cases of despotic favourites were recalled. In March 1763, when John Wilkes reprinted an old fragment by Ben Jonson on the evildoings of the Earl of Mortimer, lover of Queen Isabella, who had ruled England through the infant Edward III, the reprint featured an ironic dedication to Bute.

Repeatedly, Bute would be accused of plotting to bring back the Stuart monarchy and his policies seen as a Jacobite plan to ensure Scottish and Stuart rule of Britain. The promotion of many Scottish figures to eminent political, military and legal positions would at another time have been interpreted as the consequence of the development of the Union. Under Bute, of course, it was all ammunition for opposition claims of a Buteite conspiracy to take over the country. Bute did not help himself, in that his administration was certainly marked by none too subtle cronyism. His greatest misfortune, however, was to come up against a figure in Wilkes, who (aided by Churchill) was to show himself a genius in the art of propaganda and self-promotion. In his hands, an unpopular and unqualified administrator was to be perceived as a malevolent tyrant.

The propaganda war started immediately after Bute's appointment on 29 May 1762, as First Lord of the Treasury. That day marked the first issue of *The Briton*, a pro-Bute paper edited by Tobias Smollett that was the mouthpiece of the new administration. At the suggestion (and with the financial aid) of Earl Temple, Wilkes replied on 5 June with the *North Briton*. The dramatist Arthur Murphy counteredered with the *Auditor*, also on the side of Bute, which first appeared on 10 June. Wilkes and Churchill won this war of the papers effortlessly, far outselling and outlasting their rivals.[9] Whilst this is not surprising (it is a thankless and in many ways a pointless task to try to write effective propaganda for a government that is widely disliked), the skill of Wilkes and Churchill in destroying the popular credibility of Bute was matched only by the dangerously libellous claims they repeatedly made. The themes of the *North Briton* sometimes varied to include other scandals, but were basically a repetition of simple points: Scottish preferment was dominating (and ruining) the country; Bute as 'favourite' had too much power, and was using it to increase his despotic (and crypto-Jacobite) grip on the nation; his administration was riddled with self-interested and incompetent cronies lining their own pockets; and the planned cessation of the Seven Years War was a disaster and a disgrace to Britain. These topics are often treated heavy-handedly, but they served their purpose in continually undermining Bute. They also formed the basic subjects of most of Churchill's remaining poetry.

Although we do not know precisely when Churchill and Wilkes became acquainted (their extant correspondence starts in June 1762), the change in Churchill's poetry after his absorption into contemporary politics is marked. Topical satire is present in all his early poems - Bute, for instance, is the target of a diatribe against vanity and pretended virtue in *Night* (ll. 143-65). But the attack is veiled, and the details vague enough to conceal his identity: Bute is satirised as a type (the venal politician) rather than an individual. As Churchill's involvement with Wilkes deepens, he does not pull his punches in this manner, and his character assassinations become more deliberately (and more provocatively) specific. The first two books of *The Ghost*, a long rambling commonplace book of a poem, were published in March 1762. Isolated moments of political satire occur, but they are not directed; by the third book, however, in October 1762, politics predominate, and when the final book appeared a year later in November 1763, the venality of Bute's administration has become the concluding subject of a poem which had commenced eighteen months earlier by celebrating its lack of any theme or direction.

From the summer of 1762, then, Churchill's work was increasingly centred upon his relationship with Wilkes, and their shared political battles. The significance of this for his poetic reputation in posterity will be returned to presently, but it is obvious that while a necessary (and largely winning) topicality of reference in his satire brought him contemporary acclaim, it would later raise charges of his poetic obsolescence from a readership remote from his subjects. His first fully charged attack upon Bute was a poem originally planned for the *North Briton*, *The Prophecy of Famine* (January 1763). This savage satire on Bute and Scotland embodies the difficulties in reading Churchill's work: the poem draws its not inconsiderable power from bringing together the worst racial stereotypes, insinuations and rumours that could be levelled at the Scottish. The modern reader is offended by the degree of vitriol that Churchill summons, and the pride with which his prejudices are displayed. Yet, it is precisely this degree of carefully controlled and structured prejudice that makes the poem a lot more than propaganda (and made it Churchill's most successful contemporary poem after *The Rosciad*). Churchill is often reprehensible in exploiting existing bigotry, but his ability to shape this material into his best poetry is disturbing precisely because it is undeniably powerful. At this time (January 1763), Churchill resigned his curacy, perhaps unsurprisingly. The incompatibility of his lifestyle and career with his ecclesiastical role had evidently led to some form of reprimand, and Zachary Pearce, Bishop of Rochester, is presumed to have had some part in Churchill's resignation.[10] He would be the subject of Churchill's poetic mockery more than once in future.

'Wilkes and Liberty'

The conclusion of *The Prophecy of Famine* berates Bute's illusory 'Peace'. The end of the Seven Years War had come with the Treaty of Paris, signed in February 1763. The Preliminaries of the Treaty were signed in November 1762 and approved by Parliament a month later, in December, but only after accusations that Bute had employed massive bribery to achieve this: Henry Fox, the Paymaster-General who had a reputation for venality, was appointed leader of the House of Commons in 1762 by Bute in order (it was suggested) to carry out his aims through underhand means. The assorted rumours surrounding the conduct of Fox and his entourage would be used repeatedly by Churchill in his poetry. Events, however, were gathering pace. By April 1763, Bute had resigned, sick of the tribulations and opprobrium attached to his role (the attempted implementation of an ill-judged cider tax in March may have accelerated his departure). Such was the mistrust of Bute that it was widely assumed that the 'favourite' would continue to wield power (not least over the king) in a backstage capacity: 'The SCOTTISH minister has indeed *retired*. Is HIS influence at an end?'[11] Thus asked Wilkes in No.45 of the *North Briton*, little suspecting that this question would be completely innocuous, when compared with the larger consequences of the latest issue of his paper.

No.45 of the *North Briton* was a criticism of the King's speech at the closing of Parliament on 19 April 1763, a speech commending the Peace of the Treaty of Paris. Wilkes's basic claim was that the speech was assumed to be written by 'the minister', meaning, of course, Bute. In attacking the speech, he was thus attacking Bute, and not the Crown. Such a distinction meant little, however: by claiming the speech to be 'the most abandoned instance of ministerial effrontery ever attempted to be imposed on mankind', Wilkes placed the monarch in an invidious position. Either George III was a puppet, unwittingly supporting such 'effrontery' by speaking it, or he was a knave, and willingly expressed his agreement with Bute's sentiments. On the following Tuesday, 26 April, the Secretary of State, Lord Halifax signed a general warrant for the arrest of 'the authors, printers and publishers of a seditious and treasonable paper, entitled the North Briton, Number 45'. It seems likely that the Government had been waiting for an opportunity to silence Wilkes for some time; the *North Briton* had offered far more seditious statements before. The arrest of George Kearsley, who was named as publisher, and Richard Balfe as the printer, led to Wilkes, who was arrested on Saturday 30 April.

The Government had erred badly, however. As Wilkes was not officially the author of the *North Briton*, a general warrant had been issued. Even when specific evidence from Kearsley and Balfe incriminated him, this evidence had not been given on oath. Furthermore, instead of issuing a new, specific warrant, the arrest still took place on the grounds of the general warrant. These were not just legal niceties: the potential misuses by any administration of a general warrant that was required to name no-one but which could lead to the arrest of anyone are obvious: such a warrant could easily represent an attack on personal liberty. Wilkes hardly had to exploit public sympathy – it was already given to him by the nature of his arrest, which was at best incompetent and questionably legal. He was eventually taken to the Tower of London. His house was searched by two Under-Secretaries of State, Philip Carteret Webb and Robert Wood, who removed a large number of papers. A writ of habeas corpus was granted, and Wilkes attended the Court of Common Pleas on the 3 April. After considering the evidence, the Court met again on April 6, and Lord Chief Justice Pratt freed Wilkes, on the grounds that his arrest was a breach of his parliamentary privilege.[12] Although it seemed that the draconian use of a general warrant was the reason for Wilkes's arrest being faulty, this was not accepted by Judge Pratt. On the other hand, Wilkes shrewdly made this seem to be the central issue of the case. His speech in Court is a brilliant example of his rhetorical utilisation of popular sentiment:

> The liberty of all the peers and gentlemen,–and (what touches me more sensibly) that of all the middling and inferior sort of people, who stand most in need of protection,–is, in my case, this day to be finally decided upon; a question of such importance, as to determine at once whether English liberty be a reality or a shadow.[13]

The symbolic effect of this was to ensure that Wilkes would gain the support of the majority of the public through his many future controversies: 'Wilkes and Liberty' became the popular cry of his cause. He was reportedly cheered home from the Court by crowds of thousands.

By the time of Churchill's next work, his already successful satire was thus even more intertwined with the momentum of Wilkes's cause. This only added to its celebrity and notoriety. The aged painter William Hogarth had ill-advisedly joined the political fray, publishing on 7 September 1762 a print entitled *The Times*. The date day after the Duke of Bedford had left to negotiate the Preliminar the Treaty of

Paris) itself implies Hogarth's message: he portrayed Bute the peacemaker as a fireman, hosing down the forces of war, yet assailed by the hoses of faction (representing the opposition, particularly Pitt and Temple). Two of Bute's assailants represent Wilkes and Churchill. Wilkes had warned Hogarth off the subject (there was absolutely no prior enmity between them), and was told in return that no likeness of himself or Churchill would be included. It therefore appears that Hogarth broke his word. Wilkes's revenge was the *North Briton* No.17 (25 September 1762), a relentless attack on Hogarth. The latter responded with a brilliant caricature of Wilkes, sketched during his appearance in the Court of Common Pleas in May 1763, which depicted him as a lascivious and grotesque parody of the idea of 'liberty'. Churchill's *An Epistle to William Hogarth* had evidently been gestating for some time, and appeared in response to the caricature in June. The final move was Hogarth's *The Bruiser* (August 1763), a print portraying Churchill as a huge bear, which was meant to draw attention to the random, scattershot and far from consistent nature of Churchill's abusive satire.

Although Churchill's poem is often savage, its assault upon the elderly Hogarth is not as extreme as it could be. In many ways, Hogarth is a springboard for an onslaught against wider Butean scandals. Churchill's abuse of Hogarth is leavened by praise of his real artistic abilities. It is an angry poem, but not as indiscriminate in its abuse as Churchill's detractors claimed (it was sometimes argued in the nineteenth century that the satire of Wilkes and Churchill had hastened Hogarth's death).[14] What it offers to an understanding of Churchill's aesthetic is a ferocious sense of the absence of public virtue or effective remedies for human corruptions. This vigorously nihilistic worldview is of the first importance in Churchill's satiric individuality.

The political storm over Wilkes's arrest had not disappeared by the autumn of 1763, though before it once again broke, Churchill had caused more public consternation by eloping with Elizabeth Carr, the 15-year-old daughter of a London tradesman. Her indignant family planned revenge upon him, though Churchill showed the disdain of a Restoration rake in dismissing such threats when writing to Wilkes.[15] It was suggested

INTRODUCTION

that Churchill might have been acting to help Elizabeth escape a marriage arranged against her will. The couple returned to London, and different accounts have her returning home before going back to Churchill, unable to stand the reproaches of her sister. Churchill's *The Conference* (November 1763), ostensibly a discussion of artistic patronage, contains what is often taken to be an apology for his actions in this matter.[16]

Churchill's infelicities were soon to be overshadowed by the return of Wilkes's problems. The fourth book of *The Ghost*, published in November, concludes with a long description of Scottish tyranny, led by Lord Chief Justice Mansfield, who would preside over Wilkes's (eventual) trial for libel in 1764. As an attempt to warn the public in advance against Mansfield's alleged duplicity, however, Churchill's satire failed spectacularly: Wilkes's imminent downfall occurred not in the courtroom but in Parliament. Throughout the summer, the appeals of three printers against their false imprisonment in the Wilkes arrest were heard, and considerable damages awarded. This was a blow to the administration, led (since the resignation of Bute in April) by George Grenville. Yet, ominously for Wilkes, his own case against Wood and Webb for illegal seizure of his property was delayed, as was Mansfield's trial of the *North Briton* for libel. Wilkes was denied legal redress and (more importantly) the publicity and momentum that a legal victory, of whatever kind or degree, would give to his cause. The value of these obstructions became clear when Wilkes went to the re-opening Commons on 15 November ready to complain of his arrest as a breach of his Parliamentary privilege; what he found instead was the session opened by a motion that (after hours of argument) voted the *North Briton* No. 45 'a false, scandalous and seditious libel'.[17]

Worse was to follow. Wilkes had used his own printing press that summer to print off a few copies of *An Essay on Woman*, a ribald parody of Pope's *Essay on Man*, probably composed a few years before by Wilkes and his friend Thomas Potter. Full of schoolboy humour and a few recently added swipes at Bute, the poem was not intended for publication. How Wilkes's enemies got hold of a copy remains a mystery, though there is strong suspicion of foul play.[18] The poem contained lewd parodies of scholarly footnotes, which were attributed jokingly to William Warburton,

Bishop of Gloucester, literary controversialist and notoriously verbose editor of Pope and Shakespeare. At the same time that Wilkes was defending his political career in the Commons, *An Essay on Woman* was produced in the House of Lords, read from and then voted a blasphemy and a breach of privilege against Warburton's person. That Wilkes's denouncers included an histrionic Warburton (who never lacked for enemies) and, hypocritically, the notoriously profligate Earl of Sandwich, Wilkes's former dissolute friend from the Hell Fire Club, may have earned Wilkes sympathy and his accusers much ridicule, but it did not alter the disastrous result of the dual attack upon him.

During the Commons' debate, Samuel Martin, MP and Treasurer of the Household of the Dowager Princess Augusta, recalled an attack upon himself in the *North Briton*, and announced the author of the paper to be 'a cowardly, malignant and scandalous scoundrel.' In a letter to Martin, Wilkes admitted authorship of the paper, and the two fought a duel in Hyde Park at midday on 16 November. Martin wounded Wilkes in the side with his second shot. It was commonly suspected that Martin's conduct was both long premeditated and government-assisted: he had been seen, for instance, practising his marksmanship diligently in the country that summer. The behaviour of Martin, along with that of Sandwich and Warburton in the Lords, and Sir Fletcher Norton (the aggressive Solicitor-General who had provided the legal evidence for the case against the *North Briton* No.45 in the Commons), was the subject of Churchill's angry next poem, *The Duellist*, published in January 1764. Appropriately for a poem written so much to the moment, it is one of Churchill's most direct works, and the vitriol it expends against Warburton would later be utilised in a subtler form.

The scene was now set for Wilkes's exile. If he stayed, he faced being thrown out of the House of Commons; furthermore, the pending legal trial against the *North Briton* was considered to be a hopeless cause after the disasters of 15 November (Churchill often refers to Wilkes as having been legally prejudged because of his denunciation in Parliament). Wilkes slipped out of the country on 24 December 1763, and would remain in France until 1768. He was expelled from the House of Commons on 19

INTRODUCTION

January 1764. The libel trial against the *North Briton* and the *Essay on Woman* took place on 21 February; Lord Mansfield (following his usual practice) directed the jury only to have to find evidence of publication, rather than proof of libel itself (a very significant difference), and Wilkes was found guilty of publication and reprinting. In his continued absence he was not sentenced, but instead outlawed on 1 November. Details of his long future career lie beyond the scope of this Introduction, but a word should be said about the consequences of Wilkes's struggle of 1763, not least because of its relevance to Churchill's work. That public support for Wilkes only increased during his difficulties is shown by the events of 3 December 1763, when the *North Briton* No.45 was due to be burnt by the public hangman at the Royal Exchange, as part of its Parliamentary condemnation. A riot broke out, and the event turned into another public condemnation of Bute. No reprisals were taken against the rioters, such was the public support for Wilkes.[19] Three days later, on 6 December, he won his case against Robert Wood, the Under Secretary, who stood accused of trespass and false seizure of papers during Wilkes's arrest in April. Judge Pratt condemned the unconstitutional principle of general warrants of arrest, and the jury awarded Wilkes £1,000. If this was a somewhat pyrrhic victory, given other developments, it did suggest the lasting legacy of the 'Wilkes and Liberty' cause. The vagaries of general warrants, and the abuses to which a government could put them, were questioned, and an important precedent set. From then onwards, a judgement could (and increasingly did) precisely define the limits of officials' powers of arrest. For many cases of writers and printers in the near future, Wilkes's victory was a vital precursor, not least for its symbolic value. The author of the most comprehensive guide to English law argues that the implications of Wilkes's victory 'added an important safeguard to the right to personal liberty'.[20]

Churchill's prolific rate of composition continued after Wilkes's departure to France. *The Duellist* had been proceeded by *The Author* (December 1763), a Popean defence of the necessity of satire in troubled times. His most unusual work, *Gotham*, was published in three books (in February, March and August, 1764). It is a departure from the satiric mode, containing discussions of colonialism, the political theory of monarchical involvement (the influential idea of the so-called 'Patriot-King'), the problems of works of abstract theology and philosophy (a common theme in the age of Pope's *Essay on Man* and Voltaire's *Candide*), and more straightforward Whig panegyric. Churchill was also still taking on Wilkes's enemies for their recent sins: *The Candidate* (May 1764) was an attempt to bring further opprobrium upon the Earl of Sandwich, who was then in the middle of an unsuccessful campaign to be made High Steward of Cambridge University (the subject also produced a short squib with the same name by Thomas Gray). *The Farewell* (July) seems to have been planned as part of Wilkes's attack upon government support for the Directors of the East India Company, who were currently feuding over the future of Bengal and their most charismatic (and controversial) figure, Robert Clive. Churchill's eventual poem is a Popean dialogue that suggests he was moving his range beyond more immediately Wilkesian subjects, though he writes with the same cynical honesty about insurmountable human problems. A more brutal satire, *The Times* (September), is a Juvenalian condemnation of homosexuality as the embodiment of decadent Englishness; to say that this hyperbolic and overwrought poem does not wear well with modern sensibilities would be a very large understatement, and its only purpose would seem to be to serve as a commonplace book of eighteenth-century homophobia. Churchill's last poem published in his lifetime, *Independence* (October), is a robust Whiggish return to the theme of the necessary defence of the realm from old Buteite enemies. Churchill died when visiting Wilkes in Boulogne, on 4 November, having been ill with a miliary fever (an illness with a measle-like rash), for five days. He was thirty-three. His friend Humphrey Cotes returned the body to Dover, where he was buried in the churchyard of St Martin-Le-Grand on 13 November 1764.

It is undoubtedly the case that Churchill's constitution had been affected by his lifestyle. We know that he had contracted syphilis in 1762, and ensuing dissipations must have taken their toll. His creative power had not dwindled, however: two fragments that were left with Wilkes and published by Churchill's brother John, his executor, in 1765, show his development in his short poetic career. *The Journey* anticipates Byron in its adoption of a pose of weary solitude in the face of a pointless and worthless world. A collection of sermons that were cobbled together presumably to make money had a 'Dedication' attached to them. Addressed to William Warburton, scourge of *An Essay on Woman* in the House of Lords, it is often seen as Churchill's masterpiece, the culmination of his attacks upon the self-serving and the hypocritical. It was an appropriate, if unintentional end to Churchill's writing.

Churchill's Poetry

In July 1763 Johnson and Boswell argued over the merits of Churchill's poetry. Johnson, the target of satire in *The Ghost* and the *North Briton*, was critical: 'He talked very contemptuously of Churchill's poetry, observing that "it had a temporary currency, only from its audacity of abuse, and being filled with living names, and that it would sink into oblivion"'. Boswell added a defensive afterthought:

> In this deprecation of Churchill's poetry I could not agree with him. It is very true that the greatest part of it is upon the topicks of the day, on which account, as it brought him great fame and profit at the time, it must proportionally slide out of the publick attention as other occasional objects succeed. But Churchill has extraordinary vigour both of thought and expression ... Let me add, that there are in his works many passages which are of a general nature; and his *Prophecy of Famine* is a poem of no ordinary merit.[21]

Johnson and Boswell were to be proved right, in that the topicality of Churchill's satire did indeed prove his Achilles' Heel. Reprinted and anthologised in the burgeoning collections of English poets into the nineteenth century, his 'extraordinary vigour' was increasingly overlooked, and he was judged as one who had subordinated his talents to Wilkes's political ends. The poems thus became viewed, as the nineteenth century went on, as obsolete records of a distant time. The charge of remoteness is harder to sustain today. If it cannot be refuted, it can also be applied to other, more canonical authors if necessary (since a high level of topical reference is hardly unique to eighteenth-century satire). Far greater writers than Churchill have been dismissed by hostile critics as obsolete and unreadable outside of their own context. Donald Greene, in defending Alexander Pope from similar charges, summed up the absurdity of their consequences if consistently applied, by pointing out the historical remoteness of the 'probably mythical ten-year siege of a small town in Asia Minor some three millennia ago'.[22]

The historical distance between Churchill's subject and every new generation of readers is only one of the reasons for his decline in critical favour. The accident of his writing at the time that he did ensured that he would be viewed (in a period inimical to a received notion of so-called 'Augustan' poetry) as one of a number of lesser writers who filled in the years between the death of Pope and the emergence of Wordsworth at the end of the century. Nineteenth-century literary historiography often worked through a sort of triumphalism, where the onset of the Romantic poets required their predecessors to be necessarily downgraded, and Churchill was the victim of many a clichéd denunciation of the 'Age of Reason' (the notion of which he had systematically ridiculed in his poetry). At best, Churchill was seen as a decadent follower of Dryden and Pope, offering an ersatz version of their satire without their skill, wit, polish or higher aims. By 1880 he was very easily dismissed as 'a petulant rhymer without a spark of the poet's imagination'.[23] This reaction is by no means atypical of responses in the nineteenth century. At most, these described Churchill as a talented poet who had wasted himself in political squabbles; usually, he was dismissed as a crude writer who had covered up his lack of talent by his topical appeal. Another example is T.S. Eliot's one glancing reference to Churchill, as part of his discussion of Samuel Johnson's poetry: 'The blundering assaults of his contemporary Churchill – a man of by no means poor abilities – do not make poetry; Churchill gives us an occasional right line, but never a right poem'.[24]

Many biographical and critical accounts stressed Churchill's speed (and alleged slovenliness) of composition. This mode of production was combined with his dissolute lifestyle: Churchill wrote in a slovenly way, it was argued, knocking out his lines for money, and carelessly cast them out into the world. At an extreme, this sort of analysis conflated his notoriously immoral way of life and his loose way of writing and thinking. These exaggerated dismissals are a sort of critical shorthand, and find their origins in Churchill's own poetical admissions. He mentions, repeatedly, in his work that he has not the requisite skill or refinement of other, more truly worthy poets. He can only write as quickly as he can, noting down his observations without wit or talent. Most of Churchill's critics before the twentieth century were unwilling to observe that this was a pose, and that when a poet admits his failure to call upon '*apt* ALLITERATION's *artful aid*', he is ironically protesting too much. In fact, Churchill's pretended ignorance on the subject of poetry is a central platform of his own peculiar aesthetic, and serves many purposes.

Although Churchill's work endlessly echoes the poetry of Dryden (who he admired deeply) and Pope (who he professed not to like at all), it is also noticeable for its significant difference from his famous predecessors. Satire needs a specific sort of narratorial character to impart its message. Whereas Pope cultivated a form of self-presentation where a high-minded poet looked down upon the follies of a world far beneath him, Churchill adopts a different tack. Churchill presents himself in his poetry as being blunt, somewhat hearty, lacking (apparently) in finesse, but basically honest, not least because of his willingness to admit his own follies and indiscretions. This down-to-earth, colloquial voice places him into the role of a typical (and not a consciously literary) observer. It has a levelling sense, and gives Churchill's satire the stamp of authenticity, as it speaks out against the iniquities of the powerful. It is a deliberately naïve voice that will not defend its own questionable conduct, but is, nevertheless, still shocked at the wealth of material for satire, as in *The Ghost*:

> But now, *Decorum* lost, I stand
> Bemus'd, a Pencil in my hand,
> And, dead to ev'ry sense of shame,
> Careless of Safety and of Fame,
> The names of Scoundrels minute down,
> And Libel more than half the Town.
>   (Bk 4, ll. 727-732)

The degree of falsehood and corruption is highlighted and made more surprising in its almost accidental discovery by a poetic persona that has no claims on exalted notions of virtue. Rather than an admission of failure and limitation, Churchill's self-criticisms create a unique poetic identity. Unlike Pope standing apart from the contagious world of duncery, Churchill admits his own follies and thus views his world from a level where the sins of the great are magnified. Furthermore, by repeatedly removing himself from the standards of contemporary poetic 'taste' through his self-denigration, Churchill empowers his sense of poetic 'plain-speaking', a device on his part that gives the impression of a good-natured and honest satiric voice, slave to no-one's agenda.

This impression is of the utmost importance in engrafting his satire with the tone of conviction that its content requires. His denials of poetic ability are part of a mode of address where apparent spontaneity and conviction are all important. Without this tone, Churchill's satire could easily have turned into virulent, petty, and extremely nasty squabbles that would demand the utmost patience to wade through. His manufactured persona helped him to present himself as a contemporary poet of relevance, immediacy and importance, and the effects can be seen by his success in his lifetime. His creation of this tone (and accompanying persona) sets him apart from Dryden and Pope; Churchill is best seen not as their less successful imitator and follower, but as a satirist who adapted their powerful tradition into his own technique.

The development of Churchill's poetic technique is related to his cultivation of a colloquial manner of address. In his first poems, Churchill uses decidedly Popean heroic couplets, marked for their regularity and careful enclosing of a statement within two lines. By the end of his short career, Churchill's poetry had become altogether more flexible, not least in its use of parenthetical remarks, asides and other apparent digressions, and in its deployment of a far more ambiguous tone of address. We can see this by looking at the beginning of the 'Dedication to the Sermons':

INTRODUCTION

> HEALTH to great GLOSTER – from a man unknown,
> Who holds thy health as dearly as his own,
> Accept this greeting – nor let modest fear
> Call up one maiden blush – I mean not here
> To wound with flatt'ry – 'tis a Villain's art,
> And suits not with the frankness of my heart.

    This opening salute to William Warburton is decidedly ambivalent. In the opening line the hyphen changes an apparently straightforward greeting into an apology for the speaker's lack of status (thus drawing attention to Warburton's supposed magnificence). The freedom with which lines are now enjambed creates the impression of the rhythms of a speaking voice, and almost every line is charged with an ironic meaning beneath the surface of its address. The second couplet manages to sound like a kindly remark on Warburton's modesty (the blush) whilst also establishing that he has something to be guilty of (his fearful blush, and the speed with which Churchill adds 'I mean not here', reassuring the Bishop that he is not going to embarrass him in public). The enjambment then alters the meaning of the last remark, as it becomes 'I mean not here/ To wound with flatt'ry', which is an apparent compliment (he will not shower Warburton with empty acclaim, or damn him with faint praise) and also a deadly insult (since there is no such praise to give the Bishop anyway, he will wound him in another way). Warburton was notorious for his almost grotesquely fulsome dedications to his works, and Churchill satirises this, appearing as a fawning sycophant whose compliments are endlessly qualified by his parenthetical additions and seeming afterthoughts. By simultaneously working on two levels of address, he praises Warburton whilst ironically denigrating him: in a sense Churchill is wounding him with flattery, as every apparently neutral or kind remark he makes is also a censure. To achieve this level of subtlety, where the surface address is contemporaneous with (and not easily separated from) the ironic undercurrent (as opposed to the two elements working through the normal antithesis of the couplet) is extraordinarily difficult. This intensely dramatic poem is the pinnacle of Churchill's short writing life, containing, in a compressed form, the ironic technique he deployed with more open ferocity in the rest of his work.

Churchill's poetic vigour was often characterised as at best heartiness, and at worst ineptitude and thoughtlessness. Yet his is a far more cunning and subtle body of work than his detractors (or even his admirers) have often claimed. At his most extreme (as in *The Prophecy of Famine*), Churchill exploits popular prejudice to the limits of offensiveness, yet draws on this ability to offend to create his most powerful effects. Elsewhere (in, for instance, the pungent *Epistle to William Hogarth*), Churchill's targets lead him to very nihilistic conclusions: the world is fundamentally dishonest, and rather than pointing out human aberrations from the norm, he is merely listing what is to be expected in the ways of greed and hypocrisy.[25] Not the least of his merits is this refusal to pretend to find lasting value or meaning in a society profoundly uncertain about the ways of 'progress', for all the expansive economic and geographical momentum that confronted its citizens. In this sense, as in many others, Churchill is an unsettling writer, which helps to explain Byron's sympathetic identification with this iconoclastic predecessor.

A Note on the Text

This edition includes approximately a third of Churchill's published poetry, and aims at providing a representative selection from all the areas of his short career. Churchill's textual problems are not particularly significant. Almost all of his poems were first published in quarto pamphlet form. His works were collected in two volumes, published in November 1763 and April 1765. After Churchill's death, John Wilkes promised to issue a fully annotated edition, a task that (typically) he failed to accomplish, leaving only a few notes. Churchill wrote and published quickly, and the success of some poems meant many new editions (which occasionally results in printers' errors). He also added to some later editions - by its eighth edition, *The Rosciad* had gained some four hundred lines - which has sometimes influenced the choice of text here.

I have generally taken the first quarto edition where possible, with some important exceptions. I have not offered variant readings from collated editions, except in cases where the sense is altered by my choice of text, or the punctuation is so eccentric as to need modification. Variant readings can be found in *The Collected Poems of Charles Churchill*, ed. Douglas Grant (Oxford: Clarendon Press, 1956). I have replaced the original square brackets that followed the initials of Churchill's targets with proper names, and changed double quotation marks to single, but the text is otherwise not modernised. Almost every edition of the last two centuries (with Grant's notable exception) has chosen to modernise, but the loss of Churchill's rhetorical effects seems unnecessary, given that these provide a good indication of how the poetry was meant to be read. Couplet poetics may be almost a dead art, but Churchill's uses of italics, capitalisation (particularly with proper names) and elision of vowels often give a vivid sense of the tone of a particular passage, or add a stress to the vehemence or irony of an attack; it is also a further support to the contention of this edition that Churchill was a more careful and deliberate writer than is often supposed.

The historical events that provide the context of Churchill's satire are explained in summary in the Introduction, though inevitably they can require extensive annotation and elucidation. Churchill is also an interestingly allusive poet, and I have tried to note his poetic borrowings, many of which have been previously overlooked. Shakespearean references are to separate editions of the *Arden Shakespeare; Paradise Lost* is quoted from the second Longman edition, ed. Alastair Fowler (Harlow: Longman, 1998). Pope's quotations are from the one-volume Twickenham edition of *The Poetry of Alexander Pope*, edited by John Butt (London: Methuen, 1963), and Dryden from the *Oxford Authors* edition, edited by Keith Walker (Oxford: Clarendon Press, 1984). I have quoted from the King James Bible when noting Churchill's scriptural references.

Although the notes try (necessarily) to steer clear of interpretation, sometimes Churchill's insinuations need to be spelled out. In drawing on historical sources, I have attempted to contrast modern scholarship with the opinions of Churchill's contemporaries, particularly Horace Walpole. Walpole's bias is obvious, yet his subjectivity is, along with his eyewitness knowledge, part of his value. Those interested should pursue these matters through the voluminous historical sources, which balance out the sometimes glaring prejudices of Churchill and Walpole, though even with their prejudices, the latter writers have the virtue of presenting history with a welcome immediacy.

Notes

1. See W. C. Brown, *Charles Churchill: Poet, Rake and Rebel* (Kansas: University of Kansas Press, 1953; rpt. New York: Greenwood Press, 1968), pp.38-9, and *The Poetical Works of Charles Churchill*, ed. William Tooke, 2nd edn, 3 vols. (London: William Pickering, 1844), 1, p.xxxii. Tooke claims that Churchill made £1,000 from *The Rosciad* and its sequel *The Apology* alone.
2. See *The Prophecy of Famine*, ll. 221-2.
3. See Brown, pp.16-17.
4. Brown, p.19.
5. See *The Poetical Works of Charles Churchill*, ed. Douglas Grant (Oxford: Clarendon Press, 1956), p.xiii, Brown, p.24.
6. Brown (p.28), dates it around late 1760 and early 1761, just before the success of *The Rosciad*.
7. See John Brewer, 'The Misfortunes of Lord Bute: a Case-Study in Eighteenth-Century Political Argument and Public Opinion', *Historical Journal* 16 (1973): 3-43 (5-9), which describes some of the extremely dangerous physical assaults that were attempted upon Bute, as well as other public insults.
8. Herbert M. Atherton, *Political Prints in the Age of Hogarth: a Study of the Ideographic Representation of Politics* (Oxford: Clarendon Press, 1974), p.209. Atherton discusses pictorial evidence of the dislike of Bute, and anti-Scottish prejudice (pp.208-27), as does Dorothy M. George, *English Political Caricature to 1792* (Oxford: Clarendon Press, 1959), pp.119-32.
9. The *Auditor* and the *Briton* both ceased publication in February 1763. Adrian Hamilton, in *The Infamous Essay on Woman* (London: André Deutsch, 1972), p.45, claims that the weekly circulation of the *North Briton* was around 2000 (a large figure when the amount of copies passed round or read in clubs is considered), compared to the *Briton's* 250. The precise authorship of the *North Briton* remains uncertain, though it is usually assumed that Wilkes wrote the majority of the issues. See Neil Schaeffer, 'Charles Churchill's Political Journalism', *Eighteenth-Century Studies*, 9 (1976): 406-428.

10. See Brown, pp.84-6.
11. The *North Briton* No.45, Saturday April 23, 1763.
12. The most detailed account of Wilkes's arrest and appeal can be found in Peter D. G. Thomas, *John Wilkes: a Friend to Liberty* (Oxford: Clarendon Press, 1996), pp.27-32.
13. *The Correspondence of John Wilkes*, ed. John Almon, 3 vols. (London, 1805), 1, p.117.
14. See Tooke, 1, pp.215-16.
15. See *The Correspondence of John Wilkes and Charles Churchill*, ed. E. H. Weatherly (New York: Columbia University Press, 1954), pp.74-5.
16. See Brown, pp.172-81, for the elopement, and *The Conference*, ll.213-36, for Churchill's repentance.
17. See Thomas, pp.41-2.
18. See Adrian Hamilton, *The Infamous Essay on Woman*, pp. 92-4, 156-8.
19. Horace Walpole, *Memoirs of the Reign of King George the Third*, ed. G. F. Russell Barker, 4 vols. (London: Lawrence and Bullen, 1894), 1, pp.262-3.
20. W. S. Holdsworth, *A History of English Law*, vol. 10 (London: Methuen, 1938), p.659. See pp.659-72 for the future legal implications in detail.
21. James Boswell, *The Life of Samuel Johnson*, ed. G. Birkbeck Hill, rev. L.F. Powell (Oxford:, 1965), p.297.
22. Donald Greene, 'An Anatomy of Pope-bashing', in *The Enduring Legacy: Alexander Pope Tercentenary Essays*, ed. Pat Rogers and G. S. Rousseau (Cambridge: Cambridge University Press, 1988), pp.241-281 (p.277).
23. *The English Poets: Selections with Critical Introductions* ed. T.H. Ward (London: Macmillan & Co, 1880), vol.3, p.389.
24. T.S. Eliot, 'Poetry in the Eighteenth Century', in *The Pelican Guide to English Literature: Volume 4, From Dryden to Johnson*, ed. Boris Ford (Harmondsworth: Penguin, 1957), pp.271-277 (p.276).
25. Critical interest in Churchill in the twentieth century was increasingly directed towards this nihilistic worldview, and Churchill's distinctive post-Popean presentation of himself. In the materials listed in Further Reading, see especially Morris Golden (1967), Thomas Lockwood (1979), pp.49-60, and Lance Bertelsen (1986), pp.216-53.

Further Reading

1. Editions:

William Tooke, *The Poetical Works of Charles Churchill*, 2nd edn, 3 vols. (London: William Pickering, 1844). [Tooke's first 2 volume edition had appeared in 1804. This revised version was savaged in a review-essay by John Forster in 1845 (see articles, below). Tooke is prolix and inaccurate, frequently misquoting and rarely attributing his sources, but he did gain some Churchill family material, and contains much fascinating, though often unverifiable, information.]

The Poetical Works of Charles Churchill, with Memoir, Critical Dissertation, and Explanatory Notes, ed. George Gilfillan (Edinburgh: James Nichol, 1855). [An eccentric edition, more notably for Gilfillan's Scottish indignation and rude footnotes than its accuracy.]

The Poems of Charles Churchill, ed. James Laver, 2 vols. (London: Eyre and Spottiswoode, 1933). [Helpfully, prints many of Wilkes's annotations to the 'Dedication to the Sermons' as notes.]

The Poetical Works of Charles Churchill, ed. Douglas Grant (Oxford: Clarendon Press, 1956). [The standard collected edition; unmodernised text, with significant textual variants.]

Selected Poems of Thomas Gray, Charles Churchill and William Cowper, ed. Katherine Turner (Harmondsworth: Penguin, 1997). [A modern selection of five poems, with brief notes.]

2. Books:

Bertelsen, Lance. *The Nonsense Club: Literature and Popular Culture, 1749-1764* (Oxford: Clarendon Press, 1986).

Brown, W. C. *Charles Churchill: Poet, Rake and Rebel* (Kansas: University of Kansas Press, 1953; rpt. New York: Greenwood Press, 1968).

Brown, W. C. *The Triumph of Form: A Study of the Later Masters of the Heroic Couplet* (Chapel Hill: University of North Carolina Press, 1948).

Carretta, Vincent. *George III and the Satirists from Hogarth to Byron* (Athens and London: University of Georgia Press, 1990).

Caretta, Vincent. *The Snarling Muse: Verbal and Visual Political Satire from Pope to Churchill* (Philadelphia: University of Pennsylvania Press, 1983).

Kernan, Alvin B. *The Plot of Satire* (Yale: Yale University Press, 1965).

Lockwood, Thomas. *Post Augustan Satire: Charles Churchill and Satirical Poetry, 1750-1800* (Seattle & London: University of Washington Press, 1979).

Paulson, Ronald. *Hogarth, His Life, Art and Times: Volume 3, Art and Politics, 1750-1764* (Cambridge: Lutterworth Press, 1993).

Rowland, John. *Faint Praise and Civil Leer: the 'Decline' of Eighteenth-Century Panegyric* (London and Toronto: Associated University Press, 1994).

Smith, Raymond J. *Charles Churchill* (Boston: Twayne, 1977).

Winters, Yvor. *Forms of Discovery* (Denver: Alan Swallow, 1962).

3. Essays and Articles:

Beatty, J. M. 'Charles Churchill's Treatment of the Couplet', *PMLA* 34 (1919): 60-69.

Beatty, J. M. 'Churchill's Influence on Minor Eighteenth-Century Satirists', *PMLA* 62 (1927): 162-176.

Beatty, J. M. 'The Political Satires of Charles Churchill', *Studies in Philology* 16 (1919): 303-333.

Beatty, J. M. 'The Battle of the Players and Poets, 1761-1766', *Modern Language Notes* 35 (1919): 449-462.

Briggs, Peter M. '"The brain, too finely wrought": Mind unminded in Churchill's Satires', *Modern Language Studies* 14 (1984), 39-53.

Brockhurst, Thomas M. 'Parson, Poet, and Beau', *Sewanee Review* 25 (1917): 469-481.

Brown, W. C. 'Charles Churchill: A Revaluation', *Studies in Philology* 40 (1943): 405-424.

Brown, W. C. 'Charles Churchill and Criticism in Transition', *Journal of English and Germanic Philology* 43 (1944): 163-169.

Fisher, Alan. 'The Stretching of Augustan Satire: Charles Churchill's Dedication to Warburton', *Journal of English and Germanic Philology* 72 (1973): 360-377.

Forster, John. 'Charles Churchill', in *Historical and Biographical Essays*, 2 vols (London: John Murray, 1858), II, pp.209-91.

Golden, Morris. 'Sterility and Eminence in the Poetry of Charles Churchill', *Journal of English and Germanic Philology* 66 (1967): 333-346.

Golden, Morris. 'Churchill's Literary Influence on Cowper', *Journal of English and Germanic Philology* 58 (1959): 655-665.

Golden, Morris. 'The Imagining Self in the Eighteenth Century', *Eighteenth-Century Studies* 3 (1969): 4-27.

Hammond, Brean S. and Malone, Martin. 'Pope and Churchill' in *Alexander Pope: Essays for the Tercentenary* ed. Colin Nicholson (Aberdeen: Aberdeen University Press, 1988), pp.22-37.

Jefferson, D. W. 'Satirical landscape: Churchill and Crabbe', *The Yearbook of English Studies* 6 (1976): 92-100.

Nichol, Don. 'Slander, Scandal and Satire', *Times Literary Supplement*, 28 January 2000:14.

Weatherly, E. H. 'Churchill's Literary Indebtedness to Pope', *Studies in Philology* 43 (1946): 59-69.

Whitford, Robert C. 'Gleanings of Churchill Bibliography', *Modern Language Notes* 47 (1928): 30-34.

4. John Wilkes and the North Briton:

Atherton, Herbert M. *Political Prints in the Age of Hogarth: a Study of the Ideographic Representation of Politics* (Oxford: Clarendon Press, 1974). [Contains much useful information on the popular context of anti-

Scottish feeling.]

Brewer, John. *Party Ideology and Popular Politics at the Accession of George III* (Cambridge: Cambridge University Press, 1976), pp.163-200. [An excellent chapter on the reasons for the popular appeal of Wilkes's politics.]

Brewer, John. 'The Misfortunes of Lord Bute: a Case-Study in Eighteenth-Century Political Argument and Public Opinion', *Historical Journal* 16 (1973): 3-43. [A very good account of the hostility to Bute, and the continuing historical debate about the efficacy of his administration.]

Hamilton, Adrian. *The Infamous Essay on Woman, or John Wilkes Seated Between Vice and Virtue* (London: Andrè Deutsch, 1972). [A reprint of the notorious poem, and a discussion of the Wilkes controversy. Contains much valuable information and reprints of prints and pamphlets.]

Nobbe, George. *The North Briton: a Study in Political Propaganda* (New York, 1939). [A detailed account of the paper and its controversies.]

Schaeffer, Neil. 'Charles Churchill's Political Journalism', *Eighteenth-Century Studies* 9 (1976), 406-428. [Important for attributing issues of the *North Briton* to Churchill's authorship.]

Thomas, Peter D. G. *John Wilkes: A Friend to Liberty* (Oxford: Clarendon Press, 1996). [The best and most detailed account of the complex prosecution of Wilkes in 1763-4.]

Walpole, Horace. *Memoirs of the Reign of King George the Third*, ed. G. F. Russell Barker, 4 vols. (London: Lawrence and Bullen, 1894). [Brilliantly acidic contemporary account, with many biased but invaluable reports and portraits.]

The Correspondence of John Wilkes and Charles Churchill, ed. E. H. Weatherly (New York: Columbia University Press, 1954). [Has a very good Introduction to the controversy.]

The Correspondence of the Late John Wilkes, ed. J. Almon, 3 vols (London, 1805). [Much material appertaining to the *North Briton*. Volume 3 contains Wilkes's sparse annotations of Churchill's poems.]

SELECTED POETRY

From THE ROSCIAD

[The conclusion, 1027-90]

    Last GARRICK came,—Behind him throng a train
Of snarling critics, ignorant as vain.

    One finds out,—'He's of stature somewhat low—
'Your hero always should be tall you know.—   1030
'True nat'ral greatness all consists in height,'
Produce your voucher, Critic.—'Sergeant Kyte.'

    Another can't forgive the paltry arts,
By which he makes his way to shallow hearts;
Mere pieces of finesse, traps for applause.—   1035
'Avaunt! unnat'ral start, affected pause.'

    For me, by Nature form'd to judge with phlegm,
I can't acquit by wholesale, nor condemn.
The best things carried to excess are wrong:
The start may be too frequent, pause too long;   1040
But, only us'd in proper time and place,
Severest judgment must allow them Grace.

    If Bunglers, form'd on Imitation's plan,
Just in the way that monkies mimic man,
Their copied scene with mangled arts disgrace,   1045
And pause and start with the same vacant face;
We join the critic laugh; those tricks we scorn

Which spoil the scenes they mean them to adorn.
   But when, from Nature's pure and genuine source,
These strokes of Acting flow with gen'rous force,   1050
When in the features all the soul's portray'd,
And passions, such as Garrick's, are display'd;
To me they seem from quickest feelings caught:
Each start is Nature; and each pause is Thought.

   When Reason yields to Passion's wild alarms,   1055
And the whole state of man is up in arms;
What, but a Critic, could condemn the Play'r
For pausing here, when Cool Sense pauses there?
Whilst, working from the Heart, the fire I trace,
And mark it strongly flaming to the Face;   1060
Whilst, in each sound, I hear the very man;
I can't catch words, and pity those who can.

   Let wits, like spiders, from the tortur'd brain
Fine-draw the critic-web with curious pain;
The gods,—a kindness I with thanks must pay,—   1065
Have form'd me of a coarser kind of clay;
Nor stung with Envy, nor with Spleen diseas'd,
A poor dull creature, still with Nature pleas'd;
Hence to thy praises, GARRICK, I agree,
And, pleas'd with Nature, must be pleas'd with Thee.   1070

   Now might I tell, how silence reign'd throughout,
And deep attention hush'd the rabble rout;
How ev'ry claimant, tortur'd with desire,
Was pale as ashes, or as red as fire:
But loose to Fame, the muse more simply acts,   1075
Rejects all flourish, and relates mere facts.

The judges, as the sev'ral parties came,
With temper heard, with Judgment weigh'd each Claim,
And, in their sentence happily agreed,
In name of both, Great SHAKESPEARE thus decreed: 1080

'If manly Sense; if Nature link'd with Art;
'If thorough knowledge of the Human Heart;
'If Pow'rs of acting vast and unconfin'd;
'If fewest Faults, with greatest Beauties join'd;
'If strong Expression, and strange Pow'rs, which lie   1085
'Within the magic circle of the Eye;
'If feelings which few hearts, like his, can know,
'And which no face so well as His can show;
'Deserve the Pref'rence;—GARRICK take the Chair,
'Nor quit it-'till Thou place an Equal there.'   1090

From THE GHOST

[Book 3, 793-820]

Horrid, *unwieldy*, without Form,
Savage, as OCEAN in a Storm,
Of *size prodigious*, in the rear,   795
That *Post of Honour*, should appear
Pomposo; *Fame* around should tell
How he a slave to int'rest fell;
How, for *Integrity* renown'd,
Which Booksellers have often found,   800
He for *Subscribers* baits his hook,
And takes their cash—but where's the Book?
No matter where—*Wise* Fear, we know,
Forbids the robbing of a Foe,
But what, to serve our private ends,   805
Forbids the cheating of our Friends?
No Man alive, who would not swear
All's *safe*, and therefore *honest* there:
For spite of all the learned say,
If we to Truth attention pay,   810
The word *Dishonesty* is meant
For nothing else but *Punishment*.
Fame too, should tell, nor heed the threat
Of Rogues, who Brother Rogues abet,
Nor tremble at the terrors hung   815
Aloft, to *make her hold her tongue*,
How to all Principles untrue,

Not fix'd to *old* friends nor to New,
He damns the Pension which he takes,
And loves the Stuart he forsakes.   820

[The Concluding Triumph of Corruption: Book 4, 1685-1934]

FREEDOM came next, but scarce was seen,   1685
When the sky, which appear'd serene
And gay before, was overcast;
Horror bestrode a foreign blast,
And from the prison of the North,
To Freedom deadly, Storms burst forth.   1690

A *Car* like those, in which, we're told,
Our wild Forefathers warr'd of old,
Loaded with Death, six Horses bear
Thro' the blank region of the air.
Too fierce for time or art to tame,   1695
They pour'd forth mingled smoke and flame
From their wide Nostrils; ev'ry steed
Was of that ancient savage breed
Which fell Geryon nurs'd; their food
The flesh of Man, their drink his blood.   1700

On the first Horses, ill-match'd pair,
This fat and sleek, *That* lean and bare,
Came ill-match'd Riders side by side,
And POVERTY was yoak'd with PRIDE:
Union most strange it must appear,   1705
Till other Unions make it clear.

Next, in the gall of bitterness,
With rage, which words can ill express,
With unforgiving rage, which springs

From a false zeal for holy things, 1710
Wearing such robes as Prophets wear,
False Prophets placed in PETER'S chair,
On which, in Characters of fire,
Shapes Antic, horrible and dire
Inwoven flam'd, where, to the view, 1715
In groups appear'd a rabble crew
Of Sainted Devils, where all round,
Vile Reliques of vile men were found,
Who, worse than Devils, from the birth
Perform'd the work of Hell on earth, 1720
Jugglers, Inquisitors, and Popes,
Pointing at *axes, wheels,* and *ropes,*
And *Engines,* fram'd on horrid plan,
Which none but the destroyer, Man
Could, to promote his selfish views, 1725
Have head to make or heart to use;
Bearing, to consecrate her tricks,
In her left hand a *Crucifix,*
Remembrance of Our dying Lord,
And in her right a *two-edg'd* Sword; 1730
Having her brows, in impious sport,
Adorn'd with words of high import,
On earth PEACE, *amongst men,* GOOD WILL,
Love *bearing,* and *forbearing* still,
All wrote in the *hearts-blood* of those 1735
Who rather Death than Falshood chose;
On her breast, (where, in days of Yore,
When God lov'd *Jews,* the HIGH-PRIEST wore
Those Oracles, which were decreed
T'instruct and guide the chosen seed) 1740
Having, with glory clad and strength,
The VIRGIN pictur'd at *full length,*
Whilst at her feet, in *small* pourtray'd,

As scarce worth notice, CHRIST was laid,
Came SUPERSTITION, fierce and fell,   1745
An Imp detested, e'en in hell;
Her Eye inflamed, her face all o'er
Foully besmear'd with human gore,
O'er heaps of mangled *Saints* She rode;
Fast at her heels DEATH proudly strode,   1750
And grimly smil'd, well-pleas'd to see
Such havock of mortality.
Close by her side, on mischief bent,
And urging on each bad intent,
To its full bearing, Savage, Wild,   1755
The Mother fit of such a child,
Striving the empire to advance
Of Sin and Death, came IGNORANCE.

   With looks, where dread command was plac'd,
And Sov'reign Pow'r by Pride disgrac'd;   1760
Where, loudly witnessing a mind
Of savage more than human kind,
Not chusing to be lov'd, but fear'd;
Mocking at right, MISRULE appear'd,
With Eyeballs glaring fiery red   1765
Enough to strike beholders dead,
Gnashing his teeth, and in a flood
Pouring corruption forth and blood
From his chaf'd jaws; without remorse
Whipping, and spurring on his horse,   1770
Whose sides, in their own blood embay'd,
E'en to the bone were open laid,
Came TYRANNY, disdaining awe,
And trampling over *Sense* and *Law*.
One thing and only one He knew,   1775
One object only would pursue:

Though Less (so low doth Passion bring)
Than man, he would be more than King.

With ev'ry argument and art
Which might corrupt the head and heart,   1780
Soothing the frenzy of his mind,
Companion meet, was FLATT'RY join'd.
Winning his carriage, ev'ry look
Employ'd, whilst it conceal'd a hook;
When simple most, most to be fear'd;   1785
Most crafty, when no craft appear'd;
His tales, no man like him could tell;
His words, which melted as they fell,
Might e'en a Hypocrite deceive,
And make an infidel believe,   1790
Wantonly cheating o'er and o'er
Those who had cheated been before:
Such FLATT'RY came, in evil hour,
Pois'ning the royal ear of pow'r;
And, grown by *Prostitution* great,   1795
Would be first Minister of State.

Within the Chariot, all alone,
High seated on a kind of throne,
With pebbles grac'd, a Figure came,
Whom Justice would, but dare not, name.   1800
Hard times when Justice, without fear
Dare not bring forth to public ear
The names of those, who dare offend
'Gainst Justice, and pervert her end;
But, if the Muse afford me grace,   1805
Description shall supply the place.

In *foreign* garments he was clad;
Sage Ermine o'er the glossy *Plaid*
Cast rev'rend honour, on his heart,
Wrought by the curious hand of Art,   1810
In silver wrought, and brighter far
Than heav'nly or than earthly Star,
Shone a *White Rose*, the Emblem dear
Of him He ever must revere,
Of that dread Lord, who, with his host   1815
Of faithful native rebels lost,
Like those black Spirits doom'd to hell,
At once from pow'r and virtue fell:
Around his clouded brows was plac'd
A *Bonnet*, most superbly grac'd   1820
With mighty *Thistles*, nor forgot
The sacred motto, *Touch me not.*

In the right-hand a sword He bore
Harder than Adamant, and more
Fatal than winds, which from the mouth   1825
Of the rough North invade the South;
The reeking blade to view presents
The blood of helpless Innocents,
And on the hilt, as meek become
As Lambs before the Shearers dumb,   1830
With downcast eye, and solemn show
Of deep unutterable woe,
Mourning the time when FREEDOM reign'd,
Fast to a rock was Justice chain'd.

In his left-hand, in wax imprest,   1835
With bells and gewgaws idly drest,
An *Image*, cast in baby mould,
He held, and seem'd o'erjoy'd to hold.

On this he fix'd his eyes; to this
Bowing, he gave the loyal kiss,   1840
And, for Rebellion fully ripe,
Seem'd to desire the ANTITYPE.
What if to that *Pretender's* foes
His greatness, nay, his life he owes,
Shall common obligations bind,   1845
And shake his constancy of mind?
Scorning such weak and petty chains,
Faithful to JAMES he still remains,
Tho' he the friend of GEORGE appear:
Dissimulation's Virtue here.   1850

   Jealous and Mean, he with a frown
Would awe, and keep all merit down;
Nor would to Truth and Justice bend,
Unless *out-bullied* by his friend;
Brave with the Coward, with the brave   1855
He is himself a Coward slave;
Aw'd by his fears, he has no heart
To take a great and open part;
Mines in a subtle train he springs,
And, secret, saps the ears of Kings;   1860
But not e'en there continues firm
'Gainst the resistance of a worm;
Born in a Country, *where the will
Of One is Law to all*, he still
Retain'd th' infection, with full aim   1865
To spread it wheresoe'er he came:
Freedom he hated, *Law* defied,
The Prostitute of Pow'r and Pride;
Law he with ease explains away,
And leads bewilder'd Sense astray;   1870
Much to the credit of his brain,

Puzzles the cause he can't maintain,
Proceeds on most familiar grounds,
And, where he can't convince, confounds;
Talents of rarest stamp and size,   1875
To Nature false, he misapplies,
And turns to poison what was sent
For purposes of nourishment.

   Paleness, not such as on his wings
The Messenger of Sickness brings,   1880
But such as takes its coward rise
From conscious baseness, conscious vice,
O'erspread his cheeks; *Disdain* and *Pride*,
To upstart Fortunes ever tied,
Scowl'd on his brow; within his eye,   1885
Insidious, lurking like a spy,
To Caution principled by Fear,
Not daring open to appear,
Lodged covert *Mischief*, *Passion* hung
On his lip quiv'ring; on his tongue   1890
Fraud dwelt at large; within his breast
All that makes Villain found a nest;
All that, on hell's completest plan,
E're join'd to damn the heart of man.

   Soon as the Car reach'd land, He rose,   1895
And with a look which might have froze
The heart's best blood, which was enough
Had hearts been made of sterner stuff
In Cities than elsewhere, to make
The very stoutest quail, and quake,   1900
He cast his baleful eyes around;
Fix'd without motion to the ground,
Fear waiting on surprize, All stood,

And Horror chill'd their curdled blood.
No more they thought of *Pomp*, no more 1905
(For they had seen his face before)
Of *Law* they thought; the cause forgot,
Whether it was or Ghost, or Plot,
Which drew them there, They All stood more
Like Statues than they were before. 1910

    What could be done? Could Art, could Force,
Or Both direct a proper course
To make this savage Monster tame,
Or send him back the way he came?
What neither Art, nor Force, nor Both 1915
Could do, a *Lord* of foreign growth,
A *Lord* to that base wretch allied
In Country, not in Vice and Pride,
Effected; from the self-same land,
(Bad news for our blaspheming band 1920
Of Scribblers, but deserving note)
The Poison came and Antidote.
Abash'd, the Monster hung his head,
And, like an empty Vision, fled;
His Train, like Virgin Snows which run, 1925
Kiss'd by the burning, bawdy Sun,
To lovesick streams, dissolv'd in Air;
Joy, who from absence seem'd more fair,
Came smiling, freed from slavish awe;
LOYALTY, LIBERTY, and LAW, 1930
Impatient of the galling chain,
And Yoke of pow'r, resum'd their reign;
And, burning with the glorious flame
Of Public Virtue, MANSFIELD came.

THE PROPHECY OF FAMINE. A SCOTS PASTORAL

Carmina tum melius, cum venerit ipse, canemus.
Dr. King, Oxon.

WHEN CUPID first instructs his darts to fly
From the sly corner of some cook-maid's eye,
The stripling raw, just enter'd in his teens,
Receives the wound, and wonders what it means;
His heart, like dripping, melts, and new desire   5
Within him stirs, each time she stirs the fire;
Trembling and blushing, he the fair one views,
And fain would speak, but can't—without a Muse.

   So to the sacred mount he takes his way,
Prunes his young wings, and tunes his infant lay,   10
His oaten reed to rural ditties frames,
To flocks and rocks, to hills and rills proclaims,
In simplest notes, and all unpolish'd strains,
The loves of nymphs, and *eke* the loves of swains.

   Clad, as your nymphs were always clad of yore,   15
In rustic weeds—a cook-maid now no more—
Beneath an aged oak LARDELLA lies—
Green moss, her couch; her canopy, the skies.
From aromatic shrubs the *roguish* gale
Steals *young* perfumes, and wafts them thro' the vale. 20
The youth, turn'd swain, and skill'd in rustic lays,
Fast by her side his am'rous descant plays.

Herds lowe, Flocks bleat, Pies chatter, Ravens scream,
And the full chorus dies a-down the stream.
The streams, with music freighted, as they pass,   25
Present the fair LARDELLA with a glass,
And ZEPHYR, to complete the love-sick plan,
Waves his light wings, and serves her for a fan.

But when maturer Judgment takes the lead,
These childish toys on Reason's altar bleed;   30
Form'd after some *great man,* whose name breeds awe,
Whose ev'ry sentence Fashion makes a law;
Who on mere credit his vain trophies rears,
And founds his merit on our servile fears;
Then we discard the workings of the heart,   35
And nature's banish'd by *mechanic* art.
Then, deeply read, our reading must be shown;
Vain is that knowledge which remains unknown.
Then OSTENTATION marches to our aid,
And *letter'd* PRIDE stalks forth in full parade;   40
Beneath their care behold the work refine,
Pointed each sentence, polish'd ev'ry line;
Trifles are dignified, and taught to wear
The robes of Antients with a Modern air;
NONSENSE with *Classic* ornaments is grac'd,   45
And passes current with the stamp of TASTE.

Then the rude THEOCRITE is ransack'd o'er,
And *courtly* MARO call'd from MINCIO's shore;
Sicilian Muses on our mountains roam,
Easy and free as if they were at home;   50
NYMPHS, NAIADS, NEREIDS, DRYADS, SATYRS, FAUNS,
Sport in our floods, and trip it o'er our lawns;
Flow'rs, which once flourish'd fair in GREECE AND ROME,
More fair revive in ENGLAND's meads to bloom;

Skies without cloud exotic suns adorn; 55
And roses blush, but blush without a thorn;
Landscapes unknown to *dowdy* Nature, rise,
And new Creations strike our wond'ring eyes.

   For bards, like these, who neither sing nor say,
Grave without thought, and without feeling gay, 60
Whose numbers in one even tenor flow,
Attun'd to pleasure, and *attun'd* to woe,
Who, if plain COMMON-SENSE her visit pays,
And mars one couplet in their happy lays,
As at some Ghost affrighted, start and stare, 65
And ask the meaning of her coming there;
For bards like these a wreath shall MASON bring,
Lin'd with the softest down of FOLLY'S wing;
In LOVE'S PAGODA shall they ever doze,
And GISBAL kindly rock them to repose; 70
My lord—to letters as to *faith* most true—
At once their patron and example too—
Shall *quaintly* fashion his love-labour'd dreams,
Sigh with sad winds, and weep with weeping streams,
Curious in grief, (for real grief, we know, 75
Is curious to dress up the tale of woe)
From the green umbrage of some DRUID'S seat
Shall his own works in his own way repeat.

   Me, whom no Muse of heav'nly birth inspires,
No judgment tempers when rash genius fires, 80
Who boast no merit but mere knack of rhyme,
Short gleams of sense, and satire out of time,
Who cannot follow where *trim* fancy leads
By *prattling* streams *o'er flow'r-empurpled* meads;
Who often, but without success, have pray'd 85
For *apt* ALLITERATION'S *artful aid;*

Who would, but cannot, with a master's skill,
Coin fine new epithets, *which mean no ill*;
Me, thus uncouth, thus ev'ry way unfit
For *pacing* poesy, and *ambling* wit, 90
TASTE with contempt beholds, nor deigns to place
Amongst the lowest of her favour'd race.

Thou, NATURE, art *my* goddess—to thy law
Myself I dedicate—*hence* slavish awe,
Which bends to fashion, and obeys the rules 95
Impos'd at first, and since observ'd by fools.
Hence those vile tricks which mar fair NATURE'S hue,
And bring the sober matron forth to view,
With all that artificial tawdry glare,
Which virtue scorns, and none but strumpets wear. 100
Sick of those pomps, those vanities, that waste
Of toil, which critics now mistake for *taste*,
Of false refinements sick, and labour'd ease,
Which Art, too thinly veil'd, forbids to please,
By Nature's charms (inglorious truth!) subdued, 105
However plain her dress, and haviour rude,
To *northern* climes my happier course I steer,
Climes where the Goddess reigns throughout the year,
Where undisturb'd by Art's *rebellious* plan,
She rules the *loyal Laird*, and *faithful Clan*. 110

To that rare soil, where virtues clust'ring grow,
What mighty blessings doth not ENGLAND owe?
What *waggon*-loads of courage, wealth and sense,
Doth each revolving day import from thence?
To us she gives, disinterested friend, 115
Faith without fraud, and STUARTS without end.
When we prosperity's rich trappings wear,
Come not her gen'rous sons and take a share?

And if, by some disastrous turn of fate,
Change should ensue, and ruin seize the state,   120
Shall we not find, safe in that hallow'd ground,
Such refuge as the HOLY MARTYR found?

Nor less our debt in SCIENCE, tho' denied
By the weak slaves of prejudice and pride:
Thence came the RAMSAY'S, names of worthy note,   125
Of whom one paints, as well as t'other wrote;
Thence HOME, disbanded from the sons of pray'r
For loving plays, tho' no *dull* DEAN was there;
Thence issued forth, at great MACPHERSON'S call,
That old, new, Epic Pastoral, FINGAL;   130
Thence MALLOCH, friend alike of Church and State,
OF CHRIST and LIBERTY, by grateful Fate
Rais'd to rewards, which, in a pious reign,
All daring *Infidels* should seek in vain;
Thence simple bards, by simple prudence taught,   135
To this wise town by simple patrons brought,
In simple manner utter simple lays,
And take, with simple pensions, simple praise.

Waft me some muse to TWEED'S inspiring stream,
Where all the little loves and graces dream;   140
Where slowly winding the dull waters creep,
And seem themselves to own the power of sleep,
Where on the surface Lead, like feathers, swims,
There let me bathe my yet unhallow'd limbs,
As once a SYRIAN bathed in JORDAN'S flood,   145
Wash off my native stains, correct that blood
Which mutinies at call of *English* pride,
And, deaf to prudence, rolls a *patriot* tide.

From solemn thought which overhangs the brow
Of patriot care, when things are—God knows how;   150
From nice trim points, where HONOUR, slave to rule,
In compliment to folly, plays the fool;
From those gay scenes, where mirth exalts his pow'r,
And easy Humour wings the laughing hour;
From those soft better moments, when desire   155
Beats high, and all the world of man's on fire,
When mutual ardours of the melting fair
More than repay us for whole years of care,
At *Friendship's* summons will my WILKES retreat,
And see, once seen before, that antient seat,   160
That *antient* seat, where majesty display'd
Her ensigns, *long before the world was made*?

Mean narrow maxims, which enslave mankind,
Ne'er from its bias warp thy settled mind.
Not dup'd by party, nor opinion's slave,   165
Those faculties which bounteous Nature gave
Thy honest spirit into practice brings,
Nor courts the smile, nor dreads the frown of Kings.
Let *rude licentious* Englishmen comply
With tumult's voice, and curse they know not why;   170
Unwilling to condemn, thy soul disdains
To wear vile faction's arbitrary chains,
And strictly weighs, in apprehension clear,
Things as they are, and not as they appear.
With thee GOOD-HUMOUR tempers lively Wit;   175
Enthron'd with JUDGMENT, CANDOUR loves to sit,
And Nature gave thee, open to distress,
A heart to pity, and a hand to bless.

Oft have I heard thee mourn the wretched lot
Of the poor, mean, despis'd, insulted *Scot*,   180

Who, might calm reason credit idle tales,
By rancour forg'd where prejudice prevails,
Or starves at home, or practises, thro' fear
Of starving, arts which damn all conscience here.
When *Scriblers*, to the charge by int'rest led, 185
The fierce *North-Briton* foaming at their head,
Pour forth invectives, deaf to candour's call,
And, injured by one alien, rail at all;
On *Northern Pisgah* when they take their stand,
To mark the weakness of that *Holy Land*, 190
With needless truths their libels to adorn,
And hang a nation up to public scorn,
Thy gen'rous soul condemns the frantic rage,
And hates the faithful, but ill-natured, page.

The *Scots* are poor, cries surly English pride; 195
True is the charge, nor by themselves denied.
Are they not then in strictest reason clear,
Who wisely come to mend their fortunes here?
If by low supple arts successful grown,
They sap'd our vigour to increase their own, 200
If, mean in want, and insolent in pow'r,
They only fawn'd, more surely to devour,
Roused by such wrongs should REASON take alarm,
And e'en the Muse for public safety arm;
But if they own ingenuous virtue's sway, 205
And follow where true honour points the way,
If they revere the hand by which they're fed,
And bless the donors for their daily bread,
Or by vast debts of higher import bound,
Are always humble, always grateful found, 210
If they, directed by PAUL'S holy pen,
Become discreetly all things to all men,
That all men may become all things to them,

Envy may hate, but justice can't condemn.
'Into our places, states, and beds they creep:' 215
They've sense to get, what we want sense to keep.

Once, be the hour accurs'd, accurs'd the place,
I ventur'd to blaspheme the chosen race.
Into those traps, which men, *call'd* PATRIOTS, laid,
By specious arts unwarily betray'd, 220
Madly I leagu'd against that sacred earth,
Vile parricide! which gave a parent birth.
But shall I meanly error's path pursue,
When heavenly TRUTH presents her friendly clue?
Once plunged in ill, shall I go farther in? 225
To make the oath was rash; to keep it, sin.
Backward I tread the paths I trod before,
And calm reflection hates what passion swore.
Converted, (blessed are the souls which know
Those pleasures which from true conversion flow, 230
Whether to reason, who now rules my breast,
Or to pure faith, like LYTTELTON and WEST)
Past crimes to expiate, be my present aim
To raise new trophies to the SCOTTISH name,
To make (what can the proudest Muse do more?) 235
E'en faction's sons her brighter worth adore,
To make her glories, stamp'd with honest rhymes,
In fullest tide roll down to latest times.

'Presumptuous wretch! and shall a *Muse* like thine,
'An *English Muse*, the meanest of the nine, 240
'Attempt a theme like this? Can her weak strain
'Expect indulgence from the mighty THANE?
'Should he from toils of government retire,
'And for a moment fan the poet's fire,
'Should he, of sciences the moral friend, 245

'Each *curious*, each *important* search suspend,
'Leave *unassisted* HILL of herbs to tell,
'And all the wonders of a *Cockle-Shell*,
'Having the Lord's good grace before his eyes,
'Would not *the* HOME step forth and gain the prize? 250
'Or if this wreath of honour might adorn
'The humble brows of one in *England* born,
'Presumptuous still thy daring must appear;
'Vain all thy tow'ring hopes, whilst I am here.'

   Thus spake a form, by silken smile, and tone   255
Dull and unvaried, for the LAUREAT known,
FOLLY'S chief friend, DECORUM'S eldest son,
In ev'ry party found, and yet of none.
This *airy substance*, this *substantial shade*,
Abash'd I heard, and with respect obey'd.   260

   From themes too lofty for a bard so mean,
Discretion beckons to an humbler scene,
The restless fever of ambition laid,
Calm I retire, and seek the sylvan shade.
Now be the *Muse* disrob'd of all her pride,   265
Be all the glare of verse by *Truth* supplied,
And if plain nature pours a simple strain,
Which BUTE may praise, and OSSIAN not disdain,
OSSIAN, *sublimest*, *simplest* Bard of all,
Whom *English Infidels*, MACPHERSON *call*,   270
Then round my head shall honour's ensigns wave,
And pensions mark me for a willing slave.

   Two Boys, whose birth, beyond all question springs
From great and glorious, tho' forgotten, kings,
Shepherds, of *Scottish* lineage, born and bred   275
On the same bleak and barren mountain's head,

By niggard nature doom'd on the same rocks
To spin out life, and starve themselves and flocks,
Fresh as the morning, which, enrob'd in mist,
The mountain's top with usual dulness kiss'd,   280
JOCKEY and SAWNEY to their labours rose;
Soon clad I ween, where nature needs no cloaths;
Where, from their youth enur'd to winter-skies,
Dress and her vain refinements they despise.

JOCKEY, whose manly, high-bon'd cheeks to crown, 285
With freckles spotted flam'd the golden down,
With mickle art could on the bagpipes play,
E'en from the rising to the setting day;
SAWNEY as long without remorse could bawl
HOME'S madrigals, and ditties from FINGAL.   290
Oft at his strains, all natural tho' rude,
The *Highland Lass* forgot her want of food,
And, whilst she *scratch'd* her lover into rest,
Sunk pleas'd, tho' hungry, on her SAWNEY'S breast.

Far as the eye could reach, no tree was seen,   295
Earth, clad in russet, scorn'd the lively green.
The plague of Locusts they secure defy,
For in three hours a grasshopper must die.
No living thing, whate'er its food, feasts there,
But the Camelion, who can feast on air.   300
No birds, except as birds of passage, flew,
No bee was known to hum, no dove to coo.
No streams as amber smooth, as amber clear,
Were seen to glide, or heard to warble here.
Rebellion's spring, which thro' the country ran,   305
Furnish'd, with bitter draughts, the steady clan.
No flow'rs embalm'd the air, but one white rose,
Which, on the tenth of June, by instinct blows,

By instinct blows at morn, and when the shades
Of drizzly eve prevail, by instinct fades. 310

   One, and but one poor solitary cave,
Too sparing of her favours, nature gave;
That one alone (hard tax on Scottish pride)
Shelter at once for man and beast supplied.
Their snares *without* entangling briers spread, 315
And thistles, arm'd against th' invader's head,
Stood in close rank, all entrance to oppose;
Thistles now held more precious than the rose.
All creatures, which, on nature's earliest plan,
Were form'd to loath, and to be loath'd by man; 320
Which ow'd their birth to nastiness and spite;
Deadly to touch, and hateful to the sight,
Creatures, which, when admitted in the ark
Their Saviour shunn'd, and rankled in the dark,
Found place *within*; marking her noisome road 325
With poison's trail, here crawl'd the bloated Toad:
There webs were spread of more than common size,
And half-starv'd spiders prey'd on half-starv'd flies;
In quest of food, Efts strove in vain to crawl;
Slugs, pinch'd with hunger, smear'd the slimy wall; 330
The cave around with hissing serpents rung;
On the damp roof unhealthy vapour hung,
And FAMINE, *by her children always known*,
As proud as poor, here fix'd her *native* throne.

   Here, for the sullen sky was overcast, 335
And summer shrunk beneath a wintry blast,
A native blast, which, arm'd with hail and rain,
Beat unrelenting on the naked swain,
The Boys for shelter made; behind, the sheep,
Of which those shepherds ev'ry day *take keep*, 340

Sickly crept on, and, with complainings rude,
On nature seem'd to call, and bleat for food.

JOCKEY.
Sith to this cave, by tempest, we're confined,
And within *ken* our flocks, under the wind,
Safe from the pelting of this perilous storm,   345
Are laid *emong* yon thistles, dry and warm,
What, Sawney, if by shepherds' art we try
To mock the rigour of this cruel sky?
What if we tune some merry *roundelay*?
Well dost thou sing, nor ill doth Jockey play.   350

SAWNEY.
Ah, Jockey, ill advisest thou, I *wis*,
To think of songs at such a time as this.
Sooner shall herbage crown these barren rocks,
Sooner shall fleeces clothe these ragged flocks,
Sooner shall want seize shepherds of the south,   355
And we forget to live from hand to mouth,
Than Sawney, out of Season, shall impart
The songs of gladness with an aching heart.

JOCKEY.
Still have I known thee for a silly swain;
Of things past help, what boots it to complain?   360
Nothing but mirth can conquer fortune's spite;
No sky is heavy if the heart be light:
Patience is sorrow's salve; what can't be cur'd,
So Donald right *areeds*, must be endur'd.

SAWNEY.
Full silly swain, I *wot*, is JOCKEY now;   365
How didst thou bear thy MAGGY'S falshood? h(

When with a foreign loon she stole away,
Didst thou forswear thy pipe, and shepherd's lay!
Where was thy boasted wisdom then, when I
Applied those proverbs, which you now apply? 370

JOCKEY.

O she was *bonny*! all the Highlands round
Was there a rival to my MAGGY found!
More precious (tho' that precious is to all)
Than the rare med'cine, which we Brimstone call,
Or that choice plant, so grateful to the nose, 375
Which, in I know not what far country, grows,
Was MAGGY unto me; dear do I rue,
A lass so fair should ever prove untrue.

SAWNEY.

Whether with pipe or song to charm the ear,
Thro' all the land did JAMIE find a peer? 380
Curs'd be that year by ev'ry honest Scot,
And in the shepherd's calendar forgot,
That fatal year when JAMIE, hapless swain,
In evil hour forsook the peaceful plain.
JAMIE, when our young Laird discreetly fled, 385
Was seiz'd, and hang'd till he was dead, dead, dead.

JOCKEY.

Full sorely may we all lament that day:
For all were losers in the deadly fray.
Five brothers had I, on the Scottish plains,
Well dost thou know were none more hopeful swains; 390
Five brothers there I lost, in manhood's pride,
Two in the field, and three on gibbets died;
Ah! silly swains, to follow war's alarms,
Ah! what hath shepherds' life to do with arms!

SAWNEY.

Mention it not—there saw I strangers clad 395
In all the honours of our ravish'd *Plaid*,
Saw the FERRARA too, our nation's pride,
Unwilling grace the awkward victor's side.
There fell our choicest youth, and from that day
Mote never Sawney tune the merry lay; 400
Bless'd those which fell! cursed those which still survive,
To mourn *fifteen* renew'd in *forty-five*.

Thus plain'd the Boys, when, from her throne of turf,
With boils emboss'd, and overgrown with scurf,
Vile humours, which, in life's corrupted well, 405
Mix'd at the birth, not abstinence could quell,
Pale FAMINE rear'd the head; her eager eyes,
Where hunger e'en to madness seem'd to rise,
Speaking aloud her throes and pangs of heart,
Strain'd to get loose, and from their orbs to start; 410
Her hollow cheeks were each a deep sunk cell,
Where wretchedness and horror lov'd to dwell;
With double rows of useless teeth supplied,
Her mouth, from ear to ear extended wide,
Which, when for want of food her entrails pin'd, 415
She op'd, and cursing swallow'd nought but wind;
All shrivell'd was her skin, and here and there,
Making their way by force, her bones lay bare;
Such filthy sight to hide from human view,
O'er her foul limbs a tatter'd Plaid she threw. 420

Cease, cried the Goddess, cease, despairing swains,
And from a parent hear what Jove ordains!

Pent in this barren corner of the isle,
Where partial fortune never deign'd to smile;

Like nature's bastards, reaping for our share 425
What was rejected by the lawful heir;
Unknown amongst the nations of the earth,
Or only known to raise contempt and mirth;
Long free, because the race of Roman braves
Thought it not worth their while to make us slaves; 430
Then into bondage by that nation brought,
Whose ruin we for ages vainly sought,
Whom still with unslack'd hate we view, and still,
The pow'r of mischief lost, retain the will;
Consider'd as the refuse of mankind, 435
A mass till the last moment left behind,
Which frugal nature doubted, as it lay,
Whether to stamp with life or throw away;
Which, form'd in haste, was planted in this nook,
But never enter'd in Creation's book; 440
Branded as traitors, who, for love of gold,
Would sell their God, as once their King they sold;
Long have we borne this mighty weight of ill,
These vile injurious taunts, and bear them still;
But times of happier note are now at hand, 445
And the full promise of a better land:
There, like the *Sons of Israel*, having trod,
For the fix'd term of years ordain'd by God,
A barren desart, we shall seize rich plains,
Where milk with honey flows, and *plenty* reigns. 450
With some few natives join'd, some pliant few,
Who worship interest, and our track pursue,
There shall we, tho' the wretched people grieve,
Ravage at large, nor ask the owners' leave.

 For us, the earth shall bring forth her increase; 455
For us, the flocks shall wear a golden fleece;
Fat Beeves shall yield us dainties not our own,

And the grape bleed a nectar yet unknown;
For our advantage shall their harvests grow,
And Scotsmen reap, what they disdain'd to sow; 460
For us, the sun shall climb the eastern hill;
For us, the rain shall fall, the dew distil;
When to our wishes Nature cannot rise,
Art shall be task'd to grant us fresh supplies.
His brawny arm shall drudging Labour strain, 465
And for our pleasure suffer daily pain;
Trade shall for us exert her utmost pow'rs,
Her's, all the toil; and all the profit, ours;
For us, the Oak shall from his native steep,
Descend, and fearless travel thro' the deep; 470
The sail of COMMERCE for our use unfurl'd,
Shall waft the treasures of each distant world;
For us, sublimer heights shall science reach,
For us, their Statesmen plot, their Churchmen preach;
Their noblest limbs of counsel we'll disjoint, 475
And, mocking, new ones of our own appoint;
Devouring War, imprison'd in the north,
Shall, at our call, in horrid pomp break forth,
And when, his chariot wheels with thunder hung,
Fell Discord braying with her brazen tongue, 480
Death in the van, with Anger, Hate, and Fear,
And Desolation stalking in the rear,
Revenge, by Justice guided, in his train,
He drives impetuous o'er the trembling plain,
Shall, at our bidding, quit his lawful prey, 485
And to meek, gentle, generous Peace give way.

   Think not, my sons, that this so bless'd estate
Stands at a distance on the roll of fate;
Already big with hopes of future sway,
E'en from this cave I scent my destined prey. 490

Think not, that this dominion o'er a race,
Whose former deeds shall time's last annals grace,
In the rough face of peril must be sought,
And with the lives of thousands dearly bought;
No—fool'd by cunning, by that happy art   495
Which laughs to scorn the blundering hero's heart,
Into the snare shall our kind neighbours fall
With open eyes, and fondly give us all.

   When ROME, to prop her sinking empire, bore
Their choicest levies to a foreign shore,   500
What if we seiz'd, like a destroying flood,
Their widow'd plains, and fill'd the realm with blood,
Gave an unbounded loose to manly rage,
And, scorning mercy, spar'd nor sex, nor age;
When, for our interest too mighty grown,   505
Monarchs of warlike bent possess'd the throne,
What if we strove divisions to foment,
And spread the flames of civil discontent,
Assisted those who 'gainst their king made head,
And gave the traitors refuge when they fled;   510
When restless GLORY bad her sons advance,
And pitch'd her standard in the fields of France,
What if disdaining oaths, an empty sound,
By which our nation never shall be bound,
Bravely we taught unmuzzled war to roam,   515
Thro' the weak land, and brought cheap laurels home;
When the bold traitors leagu'd for the defence
Of Law, Religion, Liberty, and Sense,
When they against their lawful Monarch rose,
And dar'd the Lord's Anointed to oppose,   520
What if we still rever'd the banish'd race,
And strove the Royal Vagrants to replace,
With fierce rebellions shook th' unsettled state,

And greatly dar'd, tho' cross'd by partial fate.
These facts, which might, where wisdom held the sway, 525
Awake the very stones to bar our way,
There shall be nothing, nor one trace remain
In the dull region of an English brain.
Bless'd with that *Faith* which mountains can remove,
First they shall *Dupes*, next *Saints*, last *Martyrs* prove. 530

   Already is this game of fate begun
Under the sanction of my Darling Son;
That Son, of nature, royal as his name,
Is destin'd to redeem our race from shame.
His boundless pow'r, beyond example great, 535
Shall make the rough way smooth, the crooked straight,
Shall for our ease the raging floods restrain,
And sink the mountain level to the plain.
DISCORD, whom in a cavern under ground
With massy fetters their late Patriot bound; 540
Where her own flesh the furious Hag might tear,
And vent her curses to the vacant air,
Where, that she never might be heard of more,
He planted LOYALTY to guard the door,
For better purpose shall Our Chief release, 545
Disguise her for a time, and call her PEACE.

   Lur'd by that name, fine engine of deceit,
Shall the weak ENGLISH help themselves to cheat,
To gain our love, with honours shall they grace
The old adherents of the STUART race, 550
Who pointed out, no matter by what name,
TORIES or JACOBITES, are still the same;
To soothe our rage, the temporising brood
Shall break the ties of truth and gratitude,
Against their Saviour venom'd falsehoods frame, 555

And brand with calumny their WILLIAM'S name;
To win our grace, (rare argument of wit)
To our untainted faith shall they commit
(Our faith which, in extremest perils tried,
Disdain'd, and still disdains, to change her side,)   560
That Sacred Majesty they all approve,
Who most enjoys, and best deserves their Love.

AN EPISTLE TO WILLIAM HOGARTH

Ut Pictura, Poesis.
Hor.

AMONGST the sons of men how few are known
Who dare be just to merit not their own!
Superior virtue and superior sense
To knaves and fools will always give offence;
Nay, men of real worth can scarcely bear,   5
So nice is Jealousy, a rival there.

   Be wicked as thou wilt; do all that's base,
Proclaim thyself the monster of thy race;
Let Vice and Folly thy black Soul divide,
Be proud with meanness, and be mean with pride;   10
Deaf to the voice of Faith and Honour, fall
From side to side, yet be of none at all;
Spurn all those charities, those sacred ties,
Which Nature, in her bounty, good as wise,
To work our safety, and ensure her plan,   15
Contriv'd to bind, and rivet man to man;
Lift against Virtue Pow'r's oppressive rod,
Betray thy Country, and deny thy God;
And, in one gen'ral comprehensive line,
To group, which volumes scarcely could define,   20
Whate'er of Sin and Dulness can be said,
Join to a FOX's heart a DASHWOOD's head,
Yet may'st thou pass unnotic'd in the throng,

And, free from Envy, safely sneak along.
The rigid Saint, by whom no mercy's shewn   25
To Saints whose lives are better than his own,
Shall spare thy crimes, and WIT, who never once
Forgave a Brother, shall forgive a Dunce.

    BUT should thy soul, form'd in some luckless hour,
Vile Int'rest scorn, nor madly grasp at Pow'r;   30
Should Love of Fame, in ev'ry noble mind
A brave disease, with love of Virtue join'd,
Spur thee to deeds of pith, where Courage tried
In Reason's court is amply justified;
Or, fond of knowledge, and averse to strife,   35
Should'st Thou prefer the calmer walk of life;
Should'st Thou, by pale and sickly STUDY led,
Pursue coy Science to the Fountain head;
Virtue thy guide, and Public Good thy end,
Should ev'ry thought to our improvement tend,   40
To curb the passions, to enlarge the mind,
Purge the sick weal, and humanize mankind:
Rage in her eye, and Malice in her breast,
Redoubled Horror grinning on her crest,
Fiercer each snake, and sharper ev'ry dart,   45
Quick from her cell shall madd'ning ENVY start;
Then shalt Thou find, but find, alas! too late,
How vain is worth! how short is Glory's date!
Then shalt Thou find, whilst Friends with Foes conspire
To give more proof than Virtue would desire,   50
Thy danger chiefly lies in acting well;
No crime's so great as daring to excell.

    WHILST SATIRE thus, disdaining mean controul,
Urg'd the free dictates of an honest soul,
CANDOUR, who, with the charity of *Paul*,   55

Still thinks the best, whene'er she thinks at all,
With the sweet milk of human kindness bless'd,
The furious ardour of my zeal repress'd.

   CAN'ST THOU, with more than usual warmth, she cry'd,
Thy malice to indulge, and feed thy pride,   60
Can'st Thou, severe by Nature as Thou art,
With all that wond'rous rancour in thy heart,
Delight to torture Truth ten thousand ways,
To spin detraction forth from themes of praise,
To make VICE sit, for purposes of strife,   65
And draw the Hag much larger than the life,
To make the good seem bad, the bad seem worse,
And represent our Nature as our curse?

   DOTH not humanity condemn that zeal
Which tends to aggravate and not to heal?   70
Doth not discretion warn thee of disgrace,
And danger grinning stare thee in the face?
Loud as the Drum, which spreading terror round,
From emptiness acquires the pow'r of sound,
Doth not the voice of NORTON strike thy ear,   75
And the pale MANSFIELD chill thy soul with fear?
Do'st Thou, fond man, believe thyself secure,
Because Thou'rt honest, and because Thou'rt poor?
Do'st Thou on Law and Liberty depend?
Turn, turn thy eyes, and view thy injur'd friend.   80
Art Thou beyond the ruffian gripe of Power,
When WILKES, *prejudg'd,* is sentenced to the Tow'r?
Do'st Thou by Privilege exemption claim,
When Privilege is little more than name?
Or to Prerogative (that glorious ground   85
On which State-scoundrels oft have safety found)
Dost Thou pretend, and there a sanction find,

Unpunish'd, thus to Libel human kind?

WHEN Poverty, the Poet's constant crime,
Compell'd thee, all unfit, to trade in rime, 90
Had not Romantic notions turn'd thy head,
Hadst Thou not valued Honour more than bread;
Had Int'rest, pliant Int'rest been thy guide,
And had not Prudence been debauch'd by Pride,
In flatt'ry's stream Thou would'st have dipp'd thy pen, 95
Applied to great, and not to honest men,
Nor should Conviction have seduc'd thy heart
To take the weaker, tho' the better part.

WHAT but rank Folly, for thy curse decreed,
Could into SATIRE's barren path mislead, 100
When, open to thy view, before thee lay
Soul-soothing PANEGYRIC'S flow'ry way?
There might the Muse have saunter'd at her ease,
And, pleasing others, learn'd herself to please,
Lords should have listen'd to the sugar'd treat, 105
And *Ladies,* simp'ring, own'd it vastly sweet;
Rogues, in thy prudent verse with virtue grac'd,
Fools, mark'd by thee as prodigies of Taste,
Must have forbid, pouring preferments down,
Such Wit, such Truth as thine to quit the gown. 110
Thy sacred Brethren too (for they, no less
Than Laymen, bring their off'rings to Success)
Had hail'd Thee good if great, and paid the vow
Sincere as that they pay to God; whilst Thou
In *Lawn* hadst whisper'd to a sleeping croud, 115
As dull as Rochester, and half as proud.'

PEACE, CANDOUR—wisely had'st thou said, and well,
Could Int'rest in this breast one moment dwell,

Could she, with prospect of success, oppose
The firm resolves, which from Conviction rose.   120
I cannot truckle to a Fool of State,
Nor take a favour from the man I hate.
Free leave have others by such means to shine;
I scorn their practice, they may laugh at mine.

But, in this charge, forgetful of thyself,   125
Thou hast assum'd the maxims of that Elf,
Whom God in wrath for man's dishonour fram'd,
CUNNING in Heav'n, amongst us PRUDENCE nam'd,
That *servile* PRUDENCE, which I leave to those
Who dare not be my Friends, can't be my Foes.   130

HAD I, with cruel and oppressive rimes,
Pursued, and turn'd misfortunes into crimes;
Had I, when Virtue gasping lay and low,
Join'd tyrant Vice, and added woe to woe;
Had I made Modesty in blushes speak,   135
And drawn the tear down Beauty's sacred cheek;
Had I (damn'd then) in thought debas'd my lays,
To wound that Sex, which Honour bids me praise;
Had I, from vengeance by base views betray'd,
In endless night sunk injur'd AYLIFF's shade;   140
Had I (which Satirists of mighty name,
Renown'd in rime, rever'd for *moral* fame,
Have done before, whom Justice shall pursue
In future verse) brought forth to public view
A Noble Friend, and made his foibles known,   145
Because his worth was greater than my own;
Had I spared those (so *Prudence* had decreed)
Whom, God so help me at my greatest need,
I ne'er will spare, those vipers to their King
Who smooth their looks, and flatter whilst they sting,   150

Or had I not taught patriot zeal to boast
Of Those, who flatter least, but love him most;
Had I thus sinn'd, my stubborn soul should bend
At CANDOUR'S voice, and take, as from a friend,
The deep rebuke; Myself should be the first   155
To hate myself, and stamp my Muse accurs'd.

BUT shall my arm—forbid it manly Pride,
Forbid it Reason, warring on my side—
For vengeance lifted high, the stroke forbear,
And hang suspended in the desart air;   160
Or to my trembling side unnerv'd sink down,
Palsied, forsooth, by CANDOUR'S half-made frown?
When Justice bids me on, shall I delay,
Because insipid CANDOUR bars my way?
When she, of all alike the puling friend,   165
Would disappoint my Satire's noblest end,
When she to villains would a sanction give,
And shelter those who are not fit to live,
When she would screen the guilty from a blush,
And bids me spare whom Reason bids me crush,   170
All leagues with CANDOUR proudly I resign;
She cannot be for Honour's turn, nor mine.

Yet come, cold monitor, half foe, half friend,
Whom Vice can't fear, whom Virtue can't commend,
Come, CANDOUR, by thy dull indiff'rence known,   175
Thou equal-blooded judge, Thou lukewarm drone,
Who, fashioned without feelings, dost expect
We call that Virtue, which we know Defect,
Come, and observe the Nature of our crimes,
The gross and rank complexion of the times,   180
Observe it well, and then review my plan;
Praise if you will, or censure if you can.

WHILST Vice presumptuous lords it as in sport,
And Piety is only known at Court;
Whilst wretched LIBERTY expiring lies 185
Beneath the fatal burthen of EXCISE;
Whilst nobles act, without one touch of shame,
What men of humble rank would blush to name;
Whilst Honour's plac'd in highest point of view,
Worshipp'd by those, who Justice never knew; 190
Whilst Bubbles of Distinction waste in play
The hours of rest, and blunder thro' the day;
With dice and cards opprobrious vigils keep,
Then turn to ruin empires in their sleep;
Whilst Fathers, by relentless passion led, 195
Doom worthy injur'd sons to beg their bread,
Merely with ill-got, ill-sav'd wealth to grace
An alien, abject, poor, proud, upstart race;
Whilst MARTIN flatters only to betray,
And WEBB gives up his dirty soul for pay; 200
Whilst titles serve to hush a villain's fears;
Whilst Peers are Agents made, and Agents Peers;
Whilst base betrayers are themselves betray'd,
And makers ruin'd by the thing they made;
Whilst CALCRAFT, false to God and man, for gold, 205
Like the old traitor who a Saviour sold,
To shame his Master, Friend, and Father gives;
Whilst BUTE remains in pow'r, whilst HOLLAND lives,
Can Satire want a subject, where Disdain,
By Virtue fir'd may point her sharpest strain? 210
Where, cloath'd with thunder, Truth may roll along,
And CANDOUR justify the rage of song?

SUCH Things, such Men before Thee, such an Age,
Where Rancour, great as thine, may glut her rage,

And sicken e'en to surfeit; where the pride 215
Of Satire, pouring down in fullest tide,
May spread wide vengeance round, yet all the while
Justice behold the ruin with a smile,
Whilst I, thy foe misdeem'd, cannot condemn
Nor disapprove that rage I wish to stem, 220
Wilt thou, degen'rate and corrupted, chuse
To soil the credit of thy haughty Muse?
With Fallacy, most infamous, to stain
Her Truth, and render all her anger vain?
When I beheld Thee incorrect but bold, 225
A various comment on the Stage unfold;
When Play'rs on Play'rs before thy satire fell,
And poor Reviews conspir'd thy wrath to swell;
When States and Statesmen next became thy care,
And only kings were safe if thou wast there, 230
Thy ev'ry word I weigh'd in Judgment's scale,
And in thy every word found Truth prevail.
Why dost Thou now to Falshood meanly fly?
Not even CANDOUR can forgive a lie.

 BAD as Men are, why should thy frantic rimes 235
Traffick in Slander, and invent new crimes,
Crimes which, existing only in thy mind,
Weak spleen brings forth to blacken all Mankind?
By pleasing hopes we lure the human heart
To practise Virtue, and improve in Art; 240
To thwart these ends (which proud of honest Fame,
A noble Muse would cherish and inflame)
Thy *Drudge* contrives, and in our full career
Sicklies our hopes with the pale hue of Fear;
Tells us that all our labours are in vain, 245
That what we seek, we never can obtain,
That, dead to Virtue, lost to Nature's plan,

Envy possesses the whole race of man,
That Worth is criminal, and Danger lies,
Danger extreme, in being good and wise.   250

'Tis a rank falsehood; search the world around,
There cannot be so vile a monster found
Not one so vile, on whom suspicions fall
Of that gross guilt, which you impute to all.
Approv'd by those who disobey her laws,   255
Virtue from Vice itself extorts applause.
Her very foes bear witness to her state;
They will not love her, but they cannot hate.
Hate Virtue for herself, with spite pursue
Merit for Merit's sake! might this be true   260
I would renounce my Nature with disdain,
And with the beasts that perish graze the plain.
Might this be true, had we so far fill'd up
The measure of our crimes, and from the cup
Of guilt so deeply drank, as not to find,   265
Thirsting for sin, one drop, one dreg behind,
Quick ruin must involve this flaming ball,
And Providence in Justice crush us all.
None but the damn'd, and amongst them the worst,
Those who for double guilt are doubly curs'd,   270
Can be so lost; nor can the worst of all
At once into such deep damnation fall;
By painful slow degrees they reach this crime,
Which e'en in Hell must be a work of time.

Cease then thy guilty rage, thou wayward son,   275
With the foul gall of discontent o'er run,
List to my voice—be honest, if you can,
Nor slander Nature in her fav'rite, man.
But if thy spirit, resolute in ill,

Once having err'd, persists in error still,   280
Go on at large, no longer worth my care,
And freely vent those blasphemies in air,
Which I would stamp as false, tho' on the tongue
Of Angels, the injurious slander hung.

 Dup'd by thy vanity, (that cunning elf   285
Who snares the Coxcomb to deceive himself)
Or blinded by thy rage, did'st Thou believe
That We too, coolly, would ourselves deceive?
That We, as sterling, falshood would admit,
Because 'twas season'd with some little wit?   290
When Fiction rises pleasing to the eye,
Men will believe, because they love the lie;
But Truth herself, if clouded with a frown,
Must have some solemn proof to pass her down.
Hast thou, maintaining that which must disgrace   295
And bring into contempt the human race,
Hast Thou, or can'st Thou, in Truth's sacred court,
To save thy credit, and thy cause support,
Produce one proof, make out one real ground
On which so great, so gross a charge to found?   300
Nay, dost Thou know one man (let that appear,
From wilful falshood I'll proclaim thee clear)
One man so lost, to Nature so untrue,
From whom this gen'ral charge thy rashness drew?
On this foundation shalt thou stand or fall—   305
Prove that in One, which you have charged on All.
Reason determines, and it must be done;
'Mongst men, or past, or present, name me One.

 Hogarth—I take thee, Candour, at thy word,
Accept thy proffer'd terms, and will be heard;   310
Thee have I heard with virulence declaim,

Nothing retain'd of CANDOUR but the name;
By Thee have I been charg'd in angry strains
With that mean falshood which my soul disdains—
HOGARTH stand forth—Nay hang not thus aloof—   315
Now, CANDOUR, now Thou shalt receive such proof,
Such damning proof, that henceforth Thou shalt fear
To tax my wrath, and own my conduct clear—
HOGARTH, stand forth—I dare thee to be tried
In that great Court, where Conscience must preside;   320
At that most solemn bar hold up thy hand;
Think before whom on what account you stand—
Speak, but consider well—from first to last
Review thy life, weigh ev'ry action past—
Nay, you shall have no reason to complain—   325
Take longer time, and view them o'er again—
Canst Thou remember from thy earliest youth,
And as thy God must judge Thee, speak the truth,
A single instance where, *Self* laid aside,
And Justice taking place of fear and pride,   330
Thou with an equal eye did'st GENIUS view,
And give to Merit what was Merit's due?
Genius and Merit are a sure offence,
And thy Soul sickens at the name of Sense.
Is any one so foolish to succeed,   335
On ENVY'S altar he is doom'd to bleed?
HOGARTH, a guilty pleasure in his eyes,
The place of Executioner supplies.
See how he glotes, enjoys the sacred feast,
And proves himself by cruelty a priest.   340

WHILST the weak Artist, to thy whims a slave,
Would bury all those pow'rs which Nature gave,
Would suffer blank concealment to obscure
Those rays, thy Jealousy could not endure,

To feed thy vanity would rust unknown,   345
And to secure thy credit blast his own,
In Hogarth he was sure to find a friend;
He could not fear, and therefore might commend.
But when his Spirit, roused by honest Shame,
Shook off that Lethargy, and soar'd to Fame;   350
When, with the pride of Man, resolv'd and strong,
He scorn'd those fears which did his Honour wrong,
And, on himself determin'd to rely,
Brought forth his labours to the public eye,
No Friend, in Thee, could such a Rebel know;   355
He had desert, and HOGARTH was his foe.

SOULS of a tim'rous cast, of petty name
In ENVY'S court, not yet quite dead to shame,
May some remorse, some qualms of Conscience feel,
And suffer Honour to abate their Zeal,   360
But the Man, truly and compleatly great
Allows no rule of action but his hate;
Thro' ev'ry bar he bravely breaks his way,
Passion his Principle, and Parts his prey.
Mediums in Vice and Virtue speak a mind   365
Within the pale of Temperance confin'd;
The daring Spirit scorns her narrow schemes,
And, good or bad, is always in extremes.

MAN'S practice duly weigh'd, thro' ev'ry age
On the same plan hath ENVY form'd her rage.   370
'Gainst those whom Fortune hath our rivals made,
In way of Science, and in way of Trade,
Stung with mean Jealousy she arms her spite,
First works, then views their ruin with delight.
Our HOGARTH here a grand improver shines,   375
And nobly on the gen'ral plan refines;

He, like himself, o'erleaps the servile bound;
Worth is his mark, wherever Worth is found.
Should Painters only his vast wrath suffice?
Genius in ev'ry walk is Lawful Prize: 380
'Tis a gross insult to his o'ergrown state;
His love to merit is to feel his hate.

   When WILKES, our Countryman, our common friend,
Arose his King, his Country to defend,
When tools of pow'r he bared to public view,   385
And from their holes the sneaking cowards drew,
When Rancour found it far beyond her reach
To soil his honour, and his truth impeach,
What could induce Thee, at a time and place
Where manly Foes had blush'd to shew their face,   390
To make that effort, which must damn thy name,
And sink Thee deep, deep in thy grave with shame?
Did virtue move Thee? no, 'twas Pride, rank Pride,
And if Thou had'st not done it, Thou had'st dy'd.
MALICE (who, disappointed of her end,   395
Whether to work the bane of Foe or Friend,
Preys on herself, and, driven to the Stake,
Gives Virtue that revenge she scorns to take)
Had kill'd Thee, tott'ring on life's utmost verge,
Had WILKES and LIBERTY escap'd thy scourge.   400

   WHEN that GREAT CHARTER, which our Fathers bought
With their best blood, was into question brought;
When, big with ruin, o'er each English head
Vile Slav'ry hung suspended by a thread;
When LIBERTY, all trembling and aghast,   405
Fear'd for the future, knowing what was past;
When ev'ry breast was chill'd with deep despair,
Till Reason pointed out that PRATT was there;

Lurking, most Ruffian-like, behind a screen,
So plac'd all things to see, himself unseen,   410
VIRTUE, with due contempt, saw HOGARTH stand,
The murd'rous pencil in his palsied hand.
What was the cause of Liberty to him,
Or what was Honour? let them sink or swim,
So he may gratify without control   415
The mean resentments of his selfish soul.
Let Freedom perish; if to Freedom true,
In the same ruin WILKES may perish too.

   WITH all the symptoms of assur'd decay,
With age and sickness pinch'd, and worn away,   420
Pale, quiv'ring lips, lank cheeks, and falt'ring tongue,
The Spirits out of tune, the Nerves unstrung,
Thy Body shrivell'd up, thy dim eyes sunk
Within their sockets deep, thy weak hams shrunk
The body's weight unable to sustain,   425
The stream of life scarce trembling thro' the vein,
More than half-kill'd by honest truths, which fell,
Thro' thy own fault, from men who wish'd thee well,
Canst thou, e'en thus, thy thoughts to vengeance give,
And, dead to all things else, to Malice live?   430
Hence, Dotard, to thy closet, shut thee in;
By deep repentance wash away thy sin,
From haunts of men to shame and sorrow fly,
And, on the verge of death, learn how to die.

   VAIN exhortation! wash the Ethiop white,   435
Discharge the leopard's spots, turn day to night,
Controul the course of Nature, bid the deep
Hush at thy Pygmy voice her waves to sleep,
Perform things passing strange, yet own thy art
Too weak to work a change in such a heart.   440

That ENVY which was woven in the frame
At first, will to the last remain the same.
Reason may droop, may die, but Envy's rage
Improves by time, and gathers strength from age.
Some, and not few, vain triflers with the pen,　　445
Unread, unpractis'd in the ways of men,
Tell us that ENVY, who with giant stride
Stalks thro' the vale of life by Virtue's side,
Retreats when she hath drawn her latest breath,
And calmly hears her praises after death.　　450
To such observers HOGARTH gives the lie;
Worth may be hears'd, but Envy cannot die;
Within the mansion of his gloomy breast,
A mansion suited well to such a guest,
Immortal, unimpair'd, she rears her head,　　455
And damns alike the living and the dead.

　　OFT have I known Thee, HOGARTH, weak and vain,
Thyself the idol of thy aukward strain,
Thro' the dull measure of a summer's day,
In phrase most vile, prate long long hours away,　　460
Whilst Friends with Friends all gaping sit, and gaze,
To hear a HOGARTH babble HOGARTH'S praise;
But if athwart thee Interruption came,
And mention'd with respect some Ancient's name,
Some Ancient's name, who in the days of yore　　465
The crown of Art with greatest honour wore
How have I seen thy coward cheek turn pale,
And blank confusion seize thy mangled tale?
How hath thy Jealousy to madness grown,
And deem'd his praise injurious to thy own?　　470
Then without mercy did thy wrath make way,
And Arts and Artists all became thy prey;
Then did'st Thou trample on establish'd rules,

And proudly levell'd all the antient schools,
Condemn'd those works, with praise thro' ages graced, 475
Which you had never seen, or could not taste.
'But would mankind have true Perfection shewn,
'It must be found in labours of my own.
'I dare to challenge, in one single piece,
'Th' united force of ITALY and GREECE.' 480
Thy eager hand the curtain then undrew,
And brought the boasted Master-piece to view.
Spare thy remarks—say not a single word—
The Picture seen, why is the Painter heard?
Call not up Shame and Anger in our cheeks; 485
Without a comment SIGISMUNDA speaks.

POOR SIGISMUNDA! what a Fate is thine!
DRYDEN, the great High Priest of all the Nine,
Reviv'd thy name, gave what a Muse could give,
And in his Numbers bad thy Mem'ry live; 490
Gave thee those soft sensations, which might move
And warm the coldest Anchorite to Love;
Gave thee that Virtue, which could curb desire,
Refine and Consecrate Love's headstrong fire;
Gave thee those griefs, which made the Stoic feel, 495
And call'd compassion forth from hearts of steel;
Gave thee that firmness, which our Sex may shame,
And made Man bow to Woman's juster claim;
So that our tears, which from Compassion flow,
Seem to debase thy dignity of woe. 500
But, O, how much unlike! how fall'n! how chang'd!
How much from Nature, and herself estranged!
How totally depriv'd of all the pow'rs
To shew her feelings, and awaken our's,
Doth SIGISMUNDA now devoted stand, 505
The helpless victim of a Dauber's hand!

BUT why, *my* HOGARTH, such a progress made,
So rare a Pattern for the Sign-Post trade;
In the full force, and whirlwind of thy pride,
Why was *Heroic* Painting laid aside?   510
Why is It not resum'd? thy Friends at Court,
Men all in place and pow'r, crave thy support;
Be grateful then for once, and thro' the field
Of politics, thy *Epic* Pencil wield;
Maintain the cause, which they, good lack! avow,   515
And would maintain too, but they know not how.

THROUGH every *Pannel* let thy Virtue tell
How BUTE prevail'd, how PITT and TEMPLE fell!
How ENGLAND'S sons (whom They conspir'd to bless
Against our Will, with insolent success)   520
Approve their fall, and with addresses run,
How got God knows, to hail the SCOTTISH Sun;
Point out our fame in war, when vengeance, hurl'd
From the strong arm of Justice, shook the world;
Thine, and thy Country's honour to encrease,   525
Point out the honours of succeeding Peace;
Our *Moderation*, Christian-like, display,
Shew, what we got, and what we gave away.
In Colours, dull and heavy as the tale,
Let a State-Chaos thro' the whole prevail.   530

BUT, of events regardless, whilst the Muse
Perhaps with too much heat her theme pursues;
Whilst her quick Spirits rouse at FREEDOM'S call,
And ev'ry drop of blood is turn'd to gall;
Whilst a dear Country, and an injured Friend,   535
Urge my strong anger to the bitt'rest end,
Whilst honest trophies to revenge are rais'd,
Let not One real Virtue pass unprais'd.

Justice with equal course bids Satire flow,
And loves the Virtue of her greatest foe. 540

O! that I here could that rare Virtue mean
Which scorns the rule of Envy, Pride and Spleen,
Which springs not from the labour'd Works of Art,
But hath its rise from Nature in the heart,
Which in itself with happiness is crown'd, 545
And spreads with joy the blessing all around!
But Truth forbids, and in these simple lays,
Contented with a diff'rent kind of Praise,
Must HOGARTH stand; that Praise which GENIUS gives,
In Which to latest time the *Artist* lives, 550
But not the *Man*; which, rightly understood,
May make us great, but cannot make us good.
That praise be HOGARTH'S; freely let him wear
The Wreath which GENIUS wove, and planted there.
Foe as I am, should Envy tear it down, 555
Myself would labour to replace the Crown.

IN walks of Humor, in that cast of Style
Which, probing to the quick, yet makes us smile;
In Comedy, thy nat'ral road to fame,
Nor let me call it by a meaner name, 560
Where a beginning, middle, and an end,
Are aptly joined; where parts on parts depend,
Each made for each, as bodies for their soul,
So as to form one true and perfect whole,
Where a plain story to the eye is told, 565
Which we conceive the moment we behold,
HOGARTH unrivall'd stands, and shall engage
Unrivall'd praise to the most distant age.

How could'st Thou then to Shame perversely run,
And tread that path which Nature bade Thee shun,   570
Why did ambition overleap her rules,
And thy vast parts become the sport of Fools?
By diff'rent methods diff'rent men excell;
But where is He, who can do all things well?
Humour thy Province, for some monstrous crime   575
Pride struck Thee with the frenzy of *Sublime*.
But, when the work was finish'd, could thy mind
So partial be, and to herself so blind,
What with contempt All view'd, to view with awe,
Nor see those faults which ev'ry Blockhead saw?   580
Blush, Thou vain Man, and if desire of Fame,
Founded on real Art, thy thoughts inflame,
To quick destruction SIGISMUNDA give,
And let her mem'ry die, that thine may live.

BUT should fond Candour, for her Mercy sake,   585
With pity view, and pardon this mistake;
Or should Oblivion, to thy wish most kind,
Wipe off that stain, nor leave one trace behind;
Of ARTS *despis'd*, of ARTISTS, by thy frown
Aw'd from just hopes, of rising Worth kept down,   590
Of all thy meanness thro' this mortal race,
Can'st Thou the living memory erase,
Or shall not Vengeance follow to the grave,
And give back just that measure which You gave?
With so much merit, and so much success,   595
With so much pow'r to curse, so much to bless,
Would He have been Man's friend, instead of foe,
Hogarth had been a little God below.
Why then, like savage Giants, fam'd of old,
Of whom in Scripture Story we are told,   600
Dost Thou in cruelty that strength employ,

Which Nature meant to save, not to destroy,
Why dost Thou, all in horrid pomp array'd,
Sit grinning o'er the ruins Thou hast made?
Most rank Ill-nature must applaud thy art;   605
But even Candour must condemn thy heart.

   FOR Me, who warm and zealous for my Friend,
In spite of railing thousands, will commend,
And no less warm and zealous 'gainst my foes,
Spite of commending thousands, will oppose,   610
I dare thy worst, with scorn behold thy rage,
But with an eye of Pity view thy Age,
Thy feeble Age, in which, as in a glass,
We see how Men to dissolution pass.
Thou *wretched Being*, whom, on Reason's plan,   615
So chang'd, so lost, I cannot call a Man,
What could persuade Thee, at this time of life,
To launch afresh into the Sea of Strife?
Better for Thee, scarce crawling on the earth,
Almost as much a child as at thy birth,   620
To have resign'd in peace thy parting breath,
And sunk unnotic'd in the arms of Death.
Why would thy grey grey hairs resentment brave,
Thus to go down with sorrow to the grave?
Now, by my Soul, it makes me blush to know   625
My Spirits could descend to such a foe.
Whatever cause the vengeance might provoke,
It seems rank Cowardice to give the stroke.

   SURE 'tis a curse which angry Fates impose,
To mortify man's arrogance, that Those   630
Who're fashion'd of some better sort of clay,
Much sooner than the common herd decay.
What bitter pangs must humbled GENIUS feel,

In their last hours, to view a SWIFT and STEELE?
How must ill-boding horrors fill her breast 635
When She beholds Men, mark'd above the rest
For qualities most dear, plung'd from that height,
And sunk, deep sunk, in second Childhood's night?
Are Men, indeed, such things, and are the best
More subject to this evil, than the rest, 640
To drivel out whole years of Ideot breath,
And sit the Monuments of living Death?
O, galling circumstance to human pride!
Abasing Thought, but not to be denied!
With curious Art the Brain too finely wrought, 645
Preys on herself, and is destroy'd by Thought.
Constant Attention wears the active mind,
Blots out her pow'rs, and leaves a blank behind.
But let not Youth, to insolence allied,
In heat of blood, in full career of pride, 650
Possess'd of GENIUS, with unhallow'd rage
Mock the infirmities of rev'rend age.
The greatest GENIUS to this Fate may bow;
Reynolds, in time, may be like HOGARTH now.

From THE DUELLIST

[Book 1, 147-248]

    Dark was the Night, by Fate decreed
For the contrivance of a deed
More black than common, which might make
This land from her foundations shake,   150
Might tear up Freedom by the root,
Destroy a WILKES, and fix a BUTE.

    Deep Horror held her wide domain;
The sky in sullen drops of rain
Forewept the morn, and thro' the air,   155
Which, op'ning, laid his bosom bare,
Loud Thunders roll'd, and Lightning stream'd;
The Owl at Freedom's window scream'd,
The Screech-Owl, prophet dire, whose breath
Brings sickness, and whose note is death;   160
The Church-Yard teem'd, and from the tomb,
All Sad and Silent, thro' the gloom,
The Ghosts of Men, in former times,
Whose Public Virtues were their crimes,
Indignant stalk'd; Sorrow and Rage   165
Blank'd their pale cheeks; in his own age
The prop of Freedom, HAMPDEN there
Felt after death the gen'rous care;
SIDNEY by grief from Heav'n was kept,
And for his brother Patriot wept;   170

All friends of LIBERTY, when Fate
Prepar'd to shorten WILKES'S date,
Heav'd, deeply hurt, the heart-felt groan,
And knew that wound to be their own.

    Hail, LIBERTY! a glorious word,   175
In other countries scarcely heard,
Or heard but as a thing of course,
Without or Energy or Force;
Here felt, enjoy'd, ador'd, she springs,
Far, far beyond the reach of Kings,   180
Fresh blooming from our Mother Earth;
With Pride and Joy she owns her birth
Deriv'd from us, and in return
Bids in our breasts her Genius burn;
Bids us with all those blessings live   185
Which LIBERTY alone can give,
Or nobly with that Spirit die,
Which makes Death more than Victory.

    Hail those Old Patriots, on whose tongue
Persuasion in the Senate hung,   190
Whilst They this sacred Cause maintained!
Hail those Old Chiefs, to honour train'd,
Who spread, when other methods fail'd,
War's bloody banner, and prevail'd!
Shall Men like these unmentioned sleep   195
Promiscuous with the common heap,
And (Gratitude forbid the crime)
Be carried down the stream of time
In Shoals, unnotic'd and forgot,
On LETHE'S stream, like flags, to rot?   200
No—they shall live, and each fair name,
Recorded in the book of fame,

Founded on Honour's basis, fast
As the round Earth, to ages last.
Some Virtues vanish with our breath, 205
Virtue like this lives after death.
Old Time himself, his scythe thrown by,
Himself lost in Eternity,
An everlasting crown shall twine
To make a WILKES and SIDNEY join. 210

   But should some slave-got Villain dare
Chains for his Country to prepare,
And, by his birth to Slav'ry broke,
Make her too feel the galling yoke,
May he be evermore accurs'd, 215
Amongst bad men be rank'd the worst,
May he be still himself, and still
Go on in Vice, and perfect Ill;
May his broad crimes each day increase,
Till he can't Live, nor Die in Peace, 220
May he be plunged so deep in shame,
That SANDWICH mayn't endure his name,
And hear, scarce crawling on the earth,
His children curse him for their birth;
May LIBERTY, beyond the grave, 225
Ordain him to be still a slave,
Grant him what here he most requires,
And damn him with his own desires!

   But should some Villain, in support
And zeal for a despairing Court, 230
Placing in Craft his confidence,
And making Honour a pretence
To do a deed of deepest shame,
Whilst filthy lucre is his aim;

Should such a Wretch, with sword or knife,   235
Contrive to practise 'gainst the life
Of One, who honour'd through the land,
For Freedom made a glorious stand,
Whose chief, perhaps his only crime,
Is (if plain Truth at such a time   240
May dare her sentiments to tell)
That He his country loves too well;
May He—but words are all too weak
The feelings of my heart to speak—
May He—O for a noble curse   245
Which might his very marrow pierce—
The general contempt engage,
And be the MARTIN of his age.

From GOTHAM

[Bk 1, 1-244]

FAR off (no matter whether *East* or *West*,
A real Country, or one made in jest)
Not yet by modern MANDEVILLES disgrac'd,
Nor by *Map-jobbers* wretchedly misplac'd,
There lies an Island, neither great nor small,   5
Which, for distinction sake, I GOTHAM call.

The Man who finds an unknown Country out,
By giving it a name acquires, no doubt,
A Gospel title, tho' the people there
The pious Christian thinks not worth his care.   10
Bar this pretence, and into air is hurl'd
The claim of EUROPE to the *Western World*.

Cast by a tempest on the savage coast,
Some roving Buccaneer set up a Post;
A Beam, in proper form transversely laid,   15
Of his Redeemer's Cross the figure made,
Of that Redeemer, with whose laws his life,
From first to last, had been one scene of strife;
His royal master's name thereon engrav'd,
Without more process, the whole race enslav'd,   20
Cut off that Charter they from Nature drew,
And made them Slaves to men they never knew.

Search ancient histories, consult records,
Under this title the most Christian Lords
Hold (thanks to Conscience) more than half the Ball; 25
O'erthrow this title, they have none at all.
For never yet might any Monarch dare,
Who liv'd to Truth, and breath'd a Christian air,
Pretend that Christ, (who came, we all agree,
To bless his people, and to set them free) 30
To make a Convert ever one law gave,
By which Converters made him first a slave.

Spite of the glosses of a canting Priest,
Who talks of Charity, but means a feast,
Who recommends it (whilst he seems to feel 35
The holy glowings of a real zeal)
To all his hearers, as a deed of worth,
To give them heaven, whom they have robb'd of earth,
Never shall One, One truly honest man,
Who, bless'd with LIBERTY, reveres her plan, 40
Allow one moment, that a Savage sire
Could from his wretched race, for childish hire,
By a wild grant, their All, their Freedom pass,
And sell his Country for a bit of glass.

Or grant this barb'rous right, Let SPAIN and FRANCE, 45
In Slav'ry bred, as purchasers advance,
Let them, whilst Conscience is at distance hurl'd,
With some gay bawble buy a golden world;
An ENGLISHMAN, in *charter'd* FREEDOM born,
Shall spurn the slavish merchandize, shall scorn 50
To take from others, thro' base private views,
What He himself would rather die, than lose.

Happy the Savage of those *early* times,

'Ere EUROPE'S sons were known, and EUROPE'S crimes!
Gold, cursed Gold! slept in the womb of earth,   55
Unfelt its mischiefs, as unknown its worth;
In full Content he found the truest wealth;
In Toil he found Diversion, Food, and Health;
Strange to the ease and luxury of Courts,
His Sports were Labours, and his Labours Sports;   60
His Youth was hardy, and his Old Age green;
Life's Morn was vig'rous, and her Eve serene;
No rules he held, but what were made for use,
No Arts he learn'd, nor ills which Arts produce;
False Lights he follow'd, but believ'd them true;   65
He knew not much, but liv'd to what he knew.

   Happy, thrice happy *now* the Savage race,
Since EUROPE took their *Gold*, and gave them *Grace*!
Pastors she sends to help them in their need,
Some who can't write, with others who can't read,   70
And on sure grounds the Gospel Pile to rear,
Sends *Missionary* Felons ev'ry Year;
Our Vices, with more Zeal than holy pray'rs,
She teaches them, and in return takes theirs;
Her rank Oppressions give them cause to rise,   75
Her Want of Prudence means, and Arms supplies,
Whilst her brave rage, not satisfied with life,
Rising in blood, adopts the *Scalping-knife*;
Knowledge She gives, enough to make them know
How abject is their State, how deep their Woe;   80
The Worth of Freedom strongly She explains,
Whilst She bows down, and loads their necks with Chains;
Faith too She plants, for her own ends imprest,
To make them bear the worst, and hope the best;
And whilst She teaches on vile int'rest's plan,   85
As Laws of God, the wild decrees of man,

Like P<small>HARISEES</small>, of whom the Scripture tell,
She makes them ten times more the Sons of Hell.

But whither do these grave reflections tend?
Are they design'd for any, or no end? 90
Briefly but this—to prove, that by no act
Which Nature made, that by no equal pact
'Twixt Man and Man, which might, if Justice heard,
Stand good, that by no benefits conferr'd,
Or purchase made, E<small>UROPE</small> in chains can hold 95
The Sons of I<small>NDIA</small>, and her mines of gold.
Chance led her there in an accursed hour,
She saw, and made the Country her's by pow'r;
Nor, drawn by Virtue's Love from Love of Fame,
Shall my rash Folly controvert the claim, 100
Or wish in thought that title overthrown,
Which coincides with, and involves my own.

E<small>UROPE</small> discover'd I<small>NDIA</small> first; I found
My right to Gotham on the self-same ground;
I first discover'd it, nor shall that plea 105
To Her be granted, and denied to Me.
I plead Possession, and, till one more bold
Shall drive me out, will that Possession hold.
With E<small>UROPE'S</small> rights my kindred rights I twine;
Hers be the W<small>ESTERN</small> W<small>ORLD</small>, be G<small>OTHAM</small> *Mine*. 110

Rejoice, Ye happy G<small>OTHAMITES</small>, rejoice;
Lift up your voice on high, a mighty voice,
The voice of Gladness, and on ev'ry tongue,
In Strains of gratitude, be praises hung,
The praises of so great and good a King; 115
Shall C<small>HURCHILL</small> reign, and shall not G<small>OTHAM</small> sing?
As on a Day, a high and holy Day,

Let ev'ry instrument of Music play,
Antient and *Modern*; Those which drew their birth
(Punctilios laid aside) from *Pagan* earth, 120
As well as those by *Christian* made and *Jew;*
Those known to many, and those known to few;
Those which in whim and frolic lightly float,
And those which swell the slow and solemn note;
Those which (whilst Reason stands in wonder by) 125
Make some *complexions* laugh, and others cry;
Those which, by some strange faculty of sound,
Can build walls up, and raze them to the ground;
Those, which can tear up forests by the roots,
And make brutes dance like Men, and Men like brutes; 130
Those which, whilst RIDICULE leads up the dance,
Make Clowns of MONMOUTH ape the Fops of FRANCE;
Those which, where *Lady* DULLNESS with *Lord* MAYORS
Presides, disdaining light and trifling airs,
Hallow the feast with *Psalmody*, and Those 135
Which, planted in our Churches to dispose
And lift the mind to Heaven, are disgrac'd
With what a foppish Organist calls *Taste*.
All, from the Fiddle (on which ev'ry Fool,
The pert Son of dull Sire, discharg'd from School, 140
Serves an apprenticeship in College ease,
And rises thro' the *Gamut* to degrees)
To Those which (tho' less common, not less sweet)
From fam'd *Saint Giles's,* and more fam'd *Vine-Street,*
(Where Heav'n, the utmost wish of man to grant, 145
Gave me an old House, and an older Aunt)
THORNTON, whilst HUMOUR pointed out the road
To her arch cub, hath hitch'd into an ode;
All Instruments, (attend Ye list'ning Spheres,
Attend Ye Sons of Men, and hear with ears) 150
All Instruments, (nor shall they seek one Hand

Impress'd from modern MUSIC'S *coxcomb* band)
All Instruments, *self-acted*, at my name
Shall pour forth harmony, and loud proclaim,
Loud but yet sweet, to the according globe,   155
My praises, whilst *gay* NATURE, in a robe,
A *Coxcomb Doctor's robe*, to the full sound
Keeps time, like BOYCE, and the World dances round.

Rejoice, Ye happy GOTHAMITES, rejoice!
Lift up your voice on high, a mighty voice,   160
The voice of gladness, and on ev'ry tongue,
In strains of gratitude, be praises hung,
The Praises of so great and good a King;
Shall CHURCHILL reign, and shall not GOTHAM sing?

INFANCY, straining backward from the breast,   165
Tetchy and wayward, what he loveth best
Refusing in his fits, whilst all the while
The Mother eyes the wrangler with a smile,
And the fond Father sits on t'other side,
Laughs at his moods, and views his spleen with pride, 170
Shall murmur forth my name, whilst at his hand
Nurse stands interpreter through GOTHAM'S land.

CHILDHOOD who, like an *April* morn, appears,
Sunshine and Rain, Hopes clouded o'er with fears,
Pleas'd and displeas'd by starts, in passion warm,   175
In Reason weak; who wrought into a storm,
Like to the fretful bullies of the deep,
Soon spends his rage, and cries himself asleep,
Who, with a fev'rish appetite oppress'd,
For trifles sighs, but hates them when possess'd,   180
His trembling lash suspended in the air,
Half-bent, and stroking back his long, lank hair,

Shall to his mates look up with eager glee,
And let his Top go down to prate of Me.

   YOUTH, who fierce, fickle, insolent, and vain,   185
Impatient urges on to MANHOOD's reign,
Impatient urges on, yet, with a cast
Of dear regard, looks back on CHILDHOOD past,
In the *mid-chase*, when the hot blood runs high,
And the quick spirits mount into his eye,   190
When Pleasure, which he deems his greatest wealth,
Beats in his heart, and paints his cheeks with health,
When the chaf'd Steed tugs proudly at the rein,
And, 'ere he starts, hath run o'er half the plain;
When, wing'd with fear, the Stag flies full in view,   195
And in full cry the eager hounds pursue,
Shall shout my praise to hills which shout again,
And e'en the *Huntsman* stop to cry *Amen*.

   MANHOOD, of form erect, who would not bow
Tho' Worlds should crack around him; on his brow   200
WISDOM serene, to Passion giving law,
Bespeaking Love, and yet commanding Awe;
DIGNITY into Grace by Mildness wrought;
COURAGE attemper'd and refin'd by Thought;
VIRTUE supreme enthron'd, within his breast   205
The Image of his Maker deep impress'd;
Lord of this Earth, which trembles at his Nod,
With Reason bless'd, and only less than God;
MANHOOD, tho' weeping Beauty kneels for aid,
Tho' Honour calls in Danger's form array'd,   210
Though cloath'd with sackcloth, Justice in the gates,
By wicked Elders chain'd, Redemption waits,
MANHOOD shall steal an hour, a little hour,
(Is't not a little One?) to hail my pow'r.

OLD-AGE, a *second Child*, by Nature curs'd 215
With more and greater evils than the first,
Weak, sickly, full of pains; in evry breath
Railing at life, and yet afraid of death;
Putting things off, with sage and solemn air,
From day to day, without one day to spare; 220
Without enjoyment, covetous of pelf,
Tiresome to friends, and tiresome to himself,
His faculties impair'd, his temper sour'd,
His memory of recent things devour'd
E'en with the acting, on his shatter'd brain, 225
Tho' the stale Registers of Youth remain;
From morn to evening babbling forth vain praise
Of those rare men, who lived in those rare days
When He, the Hero of his tale, was Young,
Dull Repetitions falt'ring on his tongue; 230
Praising gray hairs, sure mark of Wisdom's sway,
E'en whilst he curses time, which made him gray,
Scoffing at Youth, e'en whilst he would afford
All, but his gold, to have his Youth restored,
Shall for a moment, from himself set free, 235
Lean on his Crutch, and pipe forth praise to Me.

Rejoice, Ye happy GOTHAMITES, rejoice;
Lift up your voice on high, a mighty voice,
The voice of gladness, and on ev'ry tongue,
In strains of gratitude, be praises hung, 240
The praises of so great and good a King;
Shall CHURCHILL reign, and shall not GOTHAM sing?

Things without life shall in this Chorus join,
And, dumb to others' praise, be loud in mine.

THE FAREWELL

P. FAREWELL to Europe, and at once, farewell
To all the follies which in Europe dwell,
To Eastern India now, a richer clime,
Richer alas in ev'ry thing but Rime,
The Muses steer their course; and, fond of change,   5
At large, in other Worlds, desire to range,
Resolv'd at least since They the fool must play,
To do it in a diff'rent place, and way.

F. What whim is this, what errour of the brain,
What madness worse than in the dog-star's reign?   10
Why into foreign countries would You roam,
Are there not knaves and fools enough at home?
If Satire be thy object, and thy lays
As yet have shewn no talents fit for praise,
If Satire be thy object, search all round,   15
Nor to thy purpose can one spot be found
Like England, where to rampant vigour grown
Vice chokes up ev'ry Virtue, where, self-sown,
The seeds of Folly shoot forth rank and bold,
And ev'ry seed brings forth a hundred fold.   20

P. No more of this—tho' Truth (the more our shame,
The more our guilt) tho' Truth perhaps may claim,
And justify her part in this, yet here,
For the first time, e'en Truth offends my ear.
Declaim from morn to night, from night to morn,   25

Take up the theme anew, when day's new-born,
I hear, and hate—be England what She will,
With all her faults She is my Country still.

F. Thy Country, and what then? Is that mere word
Against the voice of Reason to be heard? 30
Are prejudices, deep imbib'd in youth,
To counter-act, and make thee hate the truth?
'Tis the sure symptom of a narrow soul
To draw its grand attachment from the whole,
And take up with a part; Men, not confin'd 35
Within such paltry limits, Men design'd
Their nature to exalt; where'er they go,
Wherever waves can roll, and winds can blow,
Where'er the blessed Sun, plac'd in the sky
To watch this subject world, can dart his eye, 40
Are still the same, and, prejudice out-grown,
Consider ev'ry country as their own.
At one grand view They take in Nature's plan,
Not more at home in England, than Japan.

P. My good, grave Sir of Theory, whose wit, 45
Grasping at shadows, ne'er caught substance yet,
'Tis mighty easy o'er a glass of wine
On vain refinements vainly to refine,
To laugh at poverty in plenty's reign,
To boast of Apathy when out of pain, 50
And in each sentence, worthy of the Schools,
Varnish'd with sophistry, to deal out rules
Most fit for practice, but for one poor fault
That into practice they can ne'er be brought.

At home, and sitting in your elbow-chair 55
You praise Japan, tho' you was never there.

But was the Ship this moment under sail,
Would not your mind be chang'd, your Spirits fail,
Would you not cast one longing eye to shore,
And vow to deal in such wild schemes no more?   60
Howe'er our pride may tempt us to conceal
Those passions, which we cannot chuse but feel,
There's a strange Something, which without a brain,
Fools feel, and with one wise men can't explain,
Planted in Man, to bind him to that earth,   65
In dearest ties, from whence he drew his birth.

If Honour calls, wher'er She points the way
The sons of Honour follow, and obey;
If Need compels, wherever we are sent,
'Tis want of courage not to be content;   70
But, if we have the liberty of choice,
And all depends on our own single voice,
To deem of ev'ry Country as the same
Is rank rebellion 'gainst the lawful claim
Of Nature, and such dull indifference   75
May be PHILOSOPHY, but can't be SENSE.

F. Weak and unjust Distinction, strange design,
Most peevish, most perverse, to undermine
PHILOSOPHY, and throw her empire down
By means of SENSE, from whom she holds her crown.   80
Divine PHILOSOPHY, to Thee we owe
All that is worth possessing here below;
Virtue and Wisdom consecrate thy reign,
Doubled each joy, and Pain no longer Pain.

When, like a Garden, where for want of toil   85
And wholesome discipline, the rich, rank soil
Teems with incumbrances, where all around,

Herbs noxious in their nature make the Ground,
Like the good Mother of a thankless Son,
Curse her own womb, by fruitfulness undone; 90
Like such a garden, when the human soul,
Uncultur'd, wild, impatient of controul,
Brings forth those passions of luxuriant race,
Which spread, and stifle ev'ry herb of grace,
Whilst Virtue, check'd by the cold hand of scorn, 95
Seems with'ring on the bed where she was born,
Philosophy steps in, with steady hand
She brings her aid, she clears th' encumber'd land,
Too virtuous, to spare vice one stroke, too wise
One moment to attend to Pity's cries, 100
See with what Godlike, what relentless pow'r
She roots up ev'ry weed
      P. And ev'ry flow'r.
PHILOSOPHY, a name of meek degree,
Embrac'd, in token of humility,
By the proud Sage, who, whilst he strove to hide, 105
In that vain artifice, reveal'd his pride.
PHILOSOPHY, whom Nature had design'd
To purge all errours from the human mind,
Herself misled by the Philosopher,
At once her Priest and Master, made us err; 110
Pride, Pride, like leaven in a mass of flour,
Tainted her laws, and made e'en Virtue sowre.

 Had she, content within her proper sphere,
Taught lessons suited to the human ear,
Which might fair Virtue's genuine fruits produce, 115
Made not for ornament, but real use,
The heart of Man unrival'd she had sway'd;
Prais'd by the good, and by the bad obey'd.
But when She, overturning Reason's throne,

Strove proudly in its place to plant her own; 120
When She with Apathy the breast would steel,
And teach us, deeply feeling, not to feel,
When She would wildly all her force employ,
Not to correct our passions, but destroy,
When, not content our Nature to restore, 125
As made by God, she made it new all o'er,
When, with a strange and criminal excess,
To make us more than Men, she made us less,
The Good her dwindl'd power with pity saw,
The Bad with joy, and none but fools with awe. 130

   Truth, with a simple and unvarnish'd tale,
E'en from the mouth of NORTON might prevail,
Could She get there, but Falshood's sugar'd strain
Should pour her fatal blandishments in vain,
Nor make one convert, tho' the Siren hung, 135
Where she too often hangs, on MANSFIELD's tongue.
Should all the SOPHS, whom in his course the Sun
Hath seen, or past or present, rise in One,
Should He, whilst pleasure in each sentence flows,
Like PLATO, give us Poetry in Prose, 140
Should He, full Orator, at once impart
The ATHENIAN's Genius, with the ROMAN's art;
Genius and Art should in this instance fail,
Nor Rome tho' join'd with Athens here prevail.
'Tis not in Man, 'tis not in more than man 145
To make me find one fault in Nature's plan.
Plac'd low ourselves, we censure those above,
And, wanting judgment, think that She wants love;
Blame, where we ought in reason to commend,
And think her most a foe, when most a friend. 150
Such be PHILOSOPHERS—their specious art,
Though Friendship pleads, shall never warp my heart;

Ne'er make me from this breast one passion tear,
Which Nature, my best friend, hath planted there.

F. Forgiving as a Friend, what, whilst I live, 155
As a Philosopher I can't forgive,
In this one point at last I join with You;
To Nature pay all that is Nature's due,
But let not clouded Reason sink so low,
To fancy debts she does not, cannot owe: 160
Bear, to full Manhood grown, those shackles bear
Which Nature meant us for a time to wear,
As we wear leading-strings, which, useless grown,
Are laid aside, when we can walk alone.
But on thyself, by peevish humour sway'd, 165
Wilt Thou lay burdens Nature never laid?
Wilt Thou make faults, whilst Judgment weakly errs,
And then defend, mistaking them for her's?
Dar'st Thou to say, in our enlighten'd age,
That this grand Master Passion, this brave rage, 170
Which flames out for thy country, was imprest,
And fix'd by Nature in the human breast?

If you prefer the place where you was born,
And hold all others in contempt and scorn
On fair Comparison; If on that land 175
With lib'ral, and a more than equal hand
Her gifts, as in profusion, Plenty sends;
If Virtue meets with more and better friends;
If Science finds a patron 'mongst the great;
If Honesty is Minister of State; 180
If Pow'r, the guardian of our rights design'd,
Is to that great, that only end confin'd;
If riches are employ'd to bless the poor;
If Law is sacred, Liberty secure;

Let but these facts depend on proofs of weight,   185
Reason declares, thy Love can't be too great,
And, in this light could he our Country view,
A very HOTTENTOT must love it too.

   But if by Fate's decrees, you owe your birth
To some most barren and penurious earth,   190
Where, ev'ry comfort of this life denied,
Her real wants are scantily supplied,
Where Pow'r is Reason, Liberty a Joke,
Laws never made, or made but to be broke,
To fix thy love on such a wretched spot,   195
Because in lust's wild fever, there begot,
Because, thy weight no longer fit to bear,
By chance not choice, thy Mother dropt thee there,
Is Folly, which admits not of defence;
It can't be Nature, for it is not Sense.   200
By the same argument which here you hold,
(When Falsehood's insolent, let Truth be bold)
If Propagation can in torments dwell,
A Devil must, if born there, love his hell.

   P. Had Fate, to whose decrees I lowly bend,   205
And e'en in punishment confess a friend,
Ordain'd my birth in some place yet untried,
On purpose made to mortify my pride;
Where the Sun never gave one glimpse of day,
Where Science never yet could dart one ray,   210
Had I been born on some bleak, blasted plain
Of barren Scotland, in a STUART's reign,
Or in some kingdom, where Men, weak, or worse,
Turn'd Nature's ev'ry blessing to a curse,
Where crowns of Freedom, by the fathers won,   215
Dropp'd leaf by leaf from each degen'rate Son,

In spite of all the wisdom you display,
All you have said, and yet may have to say,
My weakness here, if weakness, I confess,
I, as my country had not lov'd her less. 220

Whether strict Reason bears me out in this,
Let those who, always seeking, always miss
The ways of Reason, doubt with precious zeal;
Their's be the praise to argue, mine to feel.
Wish we to trace this passion to the root, 225
We, like a tree, may know it by its fruit,
From its rich stem ten thousand virtues spring,
Ten thousand blessings on its branches cling,
Yet in the circle of revolving years,
Not one misfortune, not one vice, appears. 230
Hence, then, and what you reason call adore;
This, if not Reason, must be something more.

But (for I wish not others to confine,
Be their opinions unrestrain'd as mine)
Whether this Love's of good, or evil growth, 235
A Vice, a Virtue, or a spice of both,
Let men of nicer argument decide;
If it is virtuous, sooth an honest pride
With lib'ral praise; if vicious, be content,
It is a Vice I never can repent; 240
A Vice, which, weigh'd in Heav'n, shall more avail
Than ten cold virtues in the other scale.

F. This wild, untemper'd zeal (which, after all,
We, Candour unimpeach'd, might madness call)
Is it a Virtue? that You scarce pretend; 245
Or can it be a Vice, like Virtue's friend,
Which draws us off from, and dissolves the force

Of private ties, nay, stops us in our course
To that grand object of the human soul,
That nobler Love which comprehends the whole.   250
Coop'd in the limits of this petty isle,
This nook, which scarce deserves a frown, or smile,
Weigh'd with Creation, You, by whim undone,
Give all your thoughts to what is scarce worth one.
The gen'rous soul, by Nature taught to soar,   255
Her strength confirm'd in Philosophic lore,
At one grand view takes in a world with ease,
And, seeing all mankind, loves all she sees.

 P. Was it most sure, which yet a doubt endures,
Not found in Reason's Creed, though found in your's 260
That these two services, like what we're told
And know of God's and Mammon's, cannot hold
And draw together, that, however loth,
We neither serve, attempting to serve both,
I could not doubt a moment which to chuse,   265
And which in common Reason to refuse.

 Invented oft for purposes of Art,
Born of the head, tho' father'd on the heart,
This grand love of the world must be confest
A barren speculation at the best.   270
Not one Man in a thousand, should he live
Beyond the usual term of life, could give,
So rare Occasion comes, and to so few,
Proof whether his regards are feign'd, or true.

 The Love we bear our Country, is a root   275
Which never fails to bring forth golden fruit,
'Tis in the mind an everlasting Spring
Of glorious actions, which become a King

Nor less become a Subject; 'tis a debt
Which bad Men, tho' they pay not, can't forget; 280
A duty which the Good delight to pay,
And ev'ry man can practise ev'ry day.

Nor, for my life (so very dim my eye,
Or dull your argument) can I descry
What you with faith assert, how that dear love 285
Which binds me to my Country, can remove
And make me of necessity forego
That gen'ral love which to the world I owe.
Those ties of private nature, small extent,
In which the mind of narrow cast is pent, 290
Are only steps on which the gen'rous soul
Mounts by degrees till She includes the whole.
That spring of Love, which in the human mind,
Founded on self, flows narrow and confin'd,
Enlarges as it rolls, and comprehends 295
The social Charities of blood, and friends,
Till smaller streams included, not o'erpast,
It rises to our Country's love at last;
And He, with lib'ral and enlarg'd mind,
Who loves his Country, cannot hate mankind. 300

F. Friend as you would appear to Common Sense,
Tell me, or think no more of a defence,
Is it a proof of love by choice to run
A vagrant from Your country?
       P. Can the son
(Shame, Shame on all such sons) with ruthless eye, 305
And heart more patient than the flint, stand by,
And by some ruffian, from all shame divorc'd,
All Virtue, see his honour'd Mother forced;
Then, no, by Him that made me, not e'en then,

Could I with patience, by the worst of Men, 310
Behold my Country plunder'd, beggar'd, lost
Beyond Redemption, all her glories cross'd,
E'en when Occasion made them ripe, her fame
Fled like a dream, while She awakes to shame.

 F. Is it not more the office of a friend, 315
The office of a Patron, to defend
Her sinking state, than basely to decline
So great a cause, and in despair resign?

 P. Beyond my reach, alas! the grievance lies,
And, whilst more able Patriots doubt, she dies. 320
From a foul source, more deep than we suppose,
Fatally deep and dark, this grievance flows.
'Tis not that Peace our glorious hopes defeats,
'Tis not the Voice of Faction in the streets,
'Tis not a gross attack on Freedom made, 325
'Tis not the arm of Privilege display'd
Against the Subject, whilst She wears no sting
To disappoint the purpose of a King,
These are no ills, or trifles, if compar'd
With those, which are contriv'd, though not declar'd. 330

 Tell me, Philosopher, is it a crime
To pry into the secret womb of Time,
Or, born in ignorance, must we despair
To reach events, and read the future there?
Why, be it so—still 'tis the right of Man, 335
Imparted by his Maker, where he can,
To former times and men his eye to cast,
And judge of what's to come, by what is past.

THE FAREWELL

    Should there be found, in some not distant year,
(O how I wish to be no Prophet here)   340
Amongst our British Lords should there be found
Some great in pow'r, in principles unsound,
Who look on Freedom with an evil eye,
In whom the springs of Loyalty are dry,
Who wish to soar on wild Ambition's wings,   345
Who hate the Commons, and who love not Kings,
Who would divide the people and the throne
To set up sep'rate int'rests of their own,
Who hate whatever aids their wholesome growth,
And only join with, to destroy them both,   350
Should there be found such men in after-times,
May Heav'n in mercy to our grievous crimes
Allot some milder vengeance, nor to them,
And to their rage this wretched land condemn.

    Thou God above, on whom all States depend,   355
Who knowest from the first their rise, and end,
If there's a day mark'd in the book of fate
When ruin must involve our equal state;
When Law, alas! must be no more, and we,
To Freedom born, must be no longer free,   360
Let not a Mob of Tyrants seize the helm,
Nor titled upstarts league to rob the realm,
Let not, whatever other ills assail,
A damned ARISTOCRACY prevail.
If, all too short, our course of Freedom run,   365
'Tis thy good pleasure we should be undone,
Let us, some comfort in our griefs to bring,
Be slaves to one, and be that one a King.

    F. Poets, accustom'd by their trade to feign,
Oft substitute creations of the brain   370

For real substance, and, themselves deceiv'd,
Would have the fiction by mankind believ'd.
Such is your case—but grant, to soothe your pride,
That You know more than all the world beside,
Why deal in hints, why make a moment's doubt,   375
Resolv'd, and like a Man, at once speak out,
Shew us our danger, tell us where it lies,
And, to ensure our safety, make us wise.

   P. Rather than bear the pain of thought, fools stray;
The Proud will rather lose than ask their way;   380
To men of Sense what needs it to unfold,
And tell a tale which they must know untold?
In the bad, Int'rest warps the canker'd heart,
The Good are hood-wink'd by the tricks of art;
And, whilst Arch, subtle Hypocrites contrive   385
To keep the flames of discontent alive,
Whilst They, with arts to honest men unknown,
Breed doubts between the People and the Throne,
Making us fear, where Reason never yet
Allow'd one fear, or could one doubt admit,   390
Themselves pass unsuspected in disguise,
And 'gainst our real danger seal our eyes.

   F. Mark them, and let their names recorded stand
On Shame's black roll, and stink thro' all the land.

   P. That might some Courage, but no Prudence be;   395
No hurt to them, and jeopardy to me.

   F. Leave out their names.
                     P. For that kind caution thanks,
But may not Judges sometimes fill up blanks?

F. Your Country's laws in doubt then you reject:

P. The Laws I love, the Lawyers I suspect: 400
Amongst twelve Judges may not One be found,
(On bare, bare possibility I ground
This wholesome doubt) who may Enlarge, Retrench,
Create, and Uncreate, and from the Bench,
With winks, smiles, nods, and such like paltry arts, 405
May work and worm into a jury's hearts,
Or, baffled there, may, turbulent of soul,
Cramp their high office, and their rights control,
Who may, tho' Judge, turn Advocate at large,
And deal replies out by the way of charge, 410
Making Interpretation all the way,
In spite of Facts, his wicked will obey,
And, leaving Law without the least defence,
May damn his Conscience to approve his Sense?

F. Whilst, the true guardians of this charter'd land, 415
In full and perfect vigour, Juries stand,
A Judge in vain shall awe, cajole, perplex.

P. Suppose I should be tried in MIDDLESEX.

F. To pack a Jury they will never dare.

P. There's no occasion to pack Juries there. 420

F. 'Gainst Prejudice all arguments are weak,
Reason herself without affect must speak.
Fly then thy Country, like a Coward fly,
Renounce her int'rest, and her laws defy.
But why, bewitch'd, to India turn thine eyes? 425
Cannot our Europe thy vast wrath suffice?

Cannot thy misbegotten Muse lay bare
Her brawny arm, and play the Butcher there?

P. Thy Counsel taken, what should Satire do?
Where could she find an object that is new?　　　430
Those travell'd Youths, whom tender Mothers wean,
And send abroad to see, and to be seen;
With whom, lest they should fornicate, or worse,
A Tutor's sent by way of a dry nurse,
Each of whom just enough of Spirit bears,　　　435
To shew our follies, and to bring home their's,
Have made all Europe's vices so well known,
They seem almost as nat'ral as our own.

F. Will India for thy purpose better do?

P. In one respect at least—there's something New.　440

F. A harmless People, in whom Nature speaks
Free and untainted, 'mongst whom Satire seeks,
But vainly seeks, so simply plain their hearts,
One bosom where to lodge her poison'd darts.

P. From knowledge speak You this, or doubt on doubt　445
Weigh'd and resolv'd, hath Reason found it out?
Neither from knowledge, nor by Reason taught,
You have Faith ev'ry where, but where You ought.
India or Europe—What's there in a name?
Propensity to vice in both the same,　　　450
Nature alike in both works for Man's good,
Alike in both by Man himself withstood.
Nabobs, as well as those who hunt them down,
Deserve a cord much better than a crown,

And a Mogul can thrones as much debase 455
As any polish'd Prince of Christian race.

F. Could You, a task more hard than You suppose,
Could You, in ridicule whilst Satire glows,
Make all their follies to the life appear,
'Tis ten to one You gain no credit here. 460
Howe'er well-drawn, the Picture after all,
Because we know not the Original,
Would not find favour in the public eye.

P. That, having your good leave, I mean to try.
And if Your observations sterling hold, 465
If the Piece should be heavy, tame, and cold,
To make it to the side of Nature lean,
And meaning nothing, something seem to mean,
To make the whole in lively colours glow,
To bring before us something that we know, 470
And from all honest men applause to win,
I'll group the Company and put them in.

F. Be that ungen'rous thought by shame suppress'd,
Add not distress to those too much distress'd.
Have They not, by blind Zeal misled, laid bare, 475
Those sores which never might endure the air?
Have They not brought their mysteries so low,
That what the Wise suspected not, Fools know?
From their first rise e'en to the present hour
Have They not prov'd their own abuse of pow'r, 480
Made it impossible, if fairly view'd,
Ever to have that dang'rous power renew'd,
Whilst, unseduc'd by Ministers, the throne
Regards our Interests, and knows its own?

P. Should ev'ry other subject chance to fail, 485
Those who have sail'd, and those who wish'd to sail
In the last Fleet, afford an ample field
Which must beyond my hopes a harvest yield.

F. On such vile food Satire can never thrive,

P. She cannot starve, if there was only CLIVE. 490

THE 'DEDICATION TO THE SERMONS'

HEALTH to great GLOSTER—from a man unknown,
Who holds thy health as dearly as his own,
Accept this greeting—nor let modest fear
Call up one maiden blush—I mean not here
To wound with flatt'ry—'tis a Villain's art, 5
And suits not with the frankness of my heart.
Truth best becomes an *Orthodox* Divine,
And, spite of hell, that Character is mine;
To speak e'en bitter truths I cannot fear;
But truth, *my Lord,* is Panegyric here. 10

    Health to great GLOSTER—nor, thro' love of ease,
Which all Priests love, let this address displease.
I ask no favour, not one note I crave,
And, when this busy brain rests in the grave,
(For till that time it never can have rest) 15
I will not trouble you with one bequest.
Some humbler Friend, my mortal journey done,
More near in blood, a Nephew or a Son,
In that dread hour Executor I'll leave;
For I, alas! have many to receive, 20
To give but little.—To great GLOSTER *Health*;
Nor let thy true and proper love of wealth
Here take a false alarm—in purse though poor,
In spirit I'm right proud, nor can endure
The mention of a bribe—thy pocket's free, 25
I, tho' a Dedicator, scorn a fee.

Let thy own offspring all thy fortunes share;
I would not ALLEN rob, nor ALLEN's heir.

Think not—a Thought unworthy thy great soul,
Which pomps of this world never could control;   30
Which never offer'd up at Pow'r's vain shrine,
Think not that Pomp and Pow'r can work on mine.
'Tis not thy Name, though that indeed is great,
'Tis not the tinsel trumpery of state,
'Tis not thy Title, Doctor tho' thou art,   35
'Tis not thy Mitre, which hath won my heart.
State is a farce; Names are but empty Things,
Degrees are bought; and, by mistaken kings,
Titles are oft misplac'd; Mitres, which shine
So bright in other eyes, are dull in mine,   40
Unless set off by Virtue; who deceives
Under the sacred sanction of *Lawn-Sleeves*,
Enhances guilt, commits a double sin;
So fair without, and yet so foul within.
'Tis not thy outward form, thy easy mien,   45
Thy sweet complacency, thy brow serene,
Thy open front, thy Love-commanding eye,
Where fifty Cupids, as in ambush, lie,
Which can from sixty to sixteen impart
The force of Love, and point his blunted dart;   50
'Tis not thy Face, tho' that by Nature's made
An index to thy soul; tho' there display'd
We see thy mind at large, and thro' thy skin
Peeps out that Courtesy which dwells within;
'Tis not thy Birth—for that is low as mine,   55
Around our heads no lineal glories shine—
But what is Birth, when, to delight mankind,
Heralds can make those arms they cannot find;
When Thou art to Thyself, thy Sire unknown,

A whole, Welch Genealogy *Alone*? 60
No, 'tis thy inward Man, thy proper Worth,
Thy right just Estimation here on earth,
Thy Life and Doctrine uniformly join'd,
And flowing from that wholesome source thy mind,
Thy known contempt of Persecution's rod, 65
Thy Charity for Man, thy Love of God,
Thy Faith in Christ, so well approv'd 'mongst men,
Which now give life, and utt'rance to my pen.
Thy Virtue, not thy Rank, demands my lays;
'Tis not the Bishop, but the Saint I praise. 70
Rais'd by that Theme, I soar on wings more strong,
And burst forth into praise with-held too long.

Much did I wish, e'en whilst I kept those sheep,
Which, for my curse, I was ordain'd to keep;
Ordain'd, alas! to keep thro' need, not choice, 75
Those sheep which never heard their shepherd's voice,
Which did not know, yet would not learn their way;
Which stray'd themselves, yet griev'd that I should stray,
Those sheep which my good Father (on his bier
Let filial duty drop the pious tear) 80
Kept well, yet starv'd himself, e'en at that time
Whilst I was pure, and innocent of rhyme;
Whilst, sacred Dullness ever in my view,
Sleep at my bidding crept from pew to pew,
Much did I wish, tho' little could I hope, 85
A Friend in him who was the Friend of Pope.

His hand, said I, my youthful steps shall guide,
And lead me safe where thousands fall beside;
His Temper, his Experience shall control,
And hush to peace the tempest of my soul; 90
His Judgment teach me, from the Critic school

How not to err, and how to err by rule;
Instruct me, mingling profit with delight,
Where Pope was wrong, where SHAKSPEARE was not right;
Where they are justly prais'd, and where thro' whim;   95
How little's due to them, how much to him.
Rais'd 'bove the slavery of common rules,
Of Common-Sense, of modern, ancient schools,
Those feelings banish'd, which mislead us all,
Fools as we are, and which we Nature call,   100
He, by his great example, might impart
A better something, and baptize it Art;
He, all the feelings of my youth forgot,
Might shew me what is Taste, by what is not;
By him supported, with a proper pride,   105
I might hold all mankind as fools beside;
He (should a World, perverse and peevish grown,
Explode his maxims and assert their own)
Might teach me, like himself, to be content,
And let their folly be their punishment;   110
Might, like himself, teach his adopted Son,
'Gainst all the World, to quote a WARBURTON.

   Fool that I was, could I so much deceive
My soul with lying hopes; could I believe
That He, the servant of his Maker sworn,   115
The servant of his Saviour, would be torn
From their embrace, and leave that dear employ,
The cure of souls, his duty and his joy,
For toys like mine, and waste his precious time,
On which so much depended, for a rime?   120
Should He forsake the task he undertook,
Desert his flock, and break his past'ral crook?
Should He (forbid it, Heav'n) so high in place,
So rich in knowledge, quit the work of Grace,

    And, idly wand'ring o'er the Muses' hill,   125
Let the salvation of mankind stand still?

    Far, far be that from Thee—yes, far from Thee
Be such revolt from Grace, and far from me
The Will to think it—Guilt is in the Thought—
Not so, Not so, hath WARBURTON been taught,   130
Not so learn'd Christ—Recall that day, well-known,
When (to maintain God's honour—and his own)
He call'd Blasphemers forth—Methinks I now
See stern Rebuke enthroned on his brow,
And arm'd with tenfold terrours—from his tongue,   135
Where fiery zeal, and Christian fury hung,
Methinks I hear the deep-ton'd thunders roll,
And chill with horrour every sinner's soul—
In vain They strive to fly—flight cannot save,
And POTTER trembles even in his grave—   140
With all the conscious pride of innocence,
Methinks I hear him, in his own defence,
Bear witness to himself, whilst all Men knew,
By Gospel-rules his witness to be true.

    O glorious Man, thy zeal I must commend,   145
Tho' it deprived me of my dearest friend.
The real motives of thy anger known,
WILKES must the justice of that anger own;
And, could thy bosom have been bar'd to view,
Pitied himself, in turn had pitied you.   150

    Bred to the law, you wisely took the gown,
Which I, like *Demas*, foolishly laid down.
Hence double strength our *Holy Mother* drew,
Me she got rid of, and made prize of you.
I, like an idle Truant, fond of play,   155

Doting on toys, and throwing gems away,
Grasping at shadows, let the substance slip;
But you, *my Lord*, renounced Attorneyship
With better purpose, and more noble aim,
And wisely played a more substantial game.   160
Nor did *Law* mourn, bless'd in her younger son,
For MANSFIELD does what GLOSTER would have done.

Doctor, Dean, Bishop, Gloster, and *My Lord*,
If haply these high Titles may accord
With thy meek Spirit; if the barren sound   165
Of pride delights Thee, to the topmost round
Of Fortune's ladder got, despise not One
For want of smooth hypocrisy undone,
Who, far below, turns up his wond'ring eye,
And, without envy, sees Thee plac'd so high: 170
Let not thy Brain (as Brains less potent might)
Dizzy, confounded, giddy with the height,
Turn round, and lose distinction, lose her skill
And wonted pow'rs of knowing good from ill,
Of sifting Truth from falshood, friends from foes;   175
Let GLOSTER well remember, how he rose,
Nor turn his back on men who made him great;
Let Him not, gorg'd with pow'r, and drunk with state,
Forget what once he was, tho' now so high;
How low, how mean, and full as poor as I.   180

Cetera desunt

Notes

Abbreviations

Boswell	James Boswell, *The Life of Samuel Johnson* ed. G. Birkbeck Hill, rev. L. F. Powell (Oxford: Oxford University Press, 1965).
Brown	W. C. Brown, *Charles Churchill: Poet, Rake and Rebel* (Kansas: University of Kansas Press, 1953; repr. New York: Greenwood Press, 1968).
DNB	*Dictionary of National Biography.*
Grant	*The Poetical Works of Charles Churchill*, ed. Douglas Grant (Oxford: Clarendon Press, 1956).
Hamilton	Adrian Hamilton, *The Infamous Essay on Woman* (London: André Deutsch, 1972).
Langford	Paul Langford, *A Polite and Commercial People: England 1727-1783* (Oxford: Oxford University Press, 1989).
OED	*Oxford English Dictionary.*
Thomas	Peter D. G. Thomas, *John Wilkes: A Friend to Liberty* (Oxford: Clarendon Press, 1996).
Tooke	*The Poetical Works of Charles Churchill*, ed. William Tooke, 2nd edn, 3 vols. (London, 1844).
Walpole	Horace Walpole, *Memoirs of the Reign of King George the Third*, ed. G. F. Russell Barker, 4 vols. (London: Lawrence and Bullen, 1894).
Correspondence	*The Correspondence of John Wilkes and Charles Churchill*, ed. E. H. Weatherly (New York: Columbia University Press, 1954).

[From *The Rosciad*]
First published in March 1761; expanded in later editions; text from the eighth edition of 1763.

The Rosciad, Churchill's first published work, is a satire on the acting and theatrical profession. The extract here is the conclusion of the poem, featuring the praising of David Garrick as the successor to Roscius, the great Roman actor whose fame gave Churchill his title.

1027. David Garrick (1717-79), after coming to London from Lichfield with his former teacher Samuel Johnson in 1737, steadily progressed in a career as actor, theatre manager and sometime dramatist and poet. Garrick's influence, as a naturalistic actor, general theatrical innovator and populariser (particularly of Shakespeare), was huge, and he dominated eighteenth-century British theatre.

1728-1036. These criticisms of Garrick are taken from a series of articles first published (under the alias 'X.Y.Z.') in *The Craftsman*; or *Gray's Inn Journal* in 1760. They were reprinted, augmented by Thaddeus Fitzpatrick's *An Enquiry into the Real Merits of a Certain Popular Performer*, later that year. Fitzpatrick, a former friend of Garrick, was in turn lampooned as 'Cock-Fribble' in Garrick's satiric rejoinder *The Fribbleriad* (1761), a poem that praises Churchill and *The Rosciad*. In 1762, Fitzpatrick helped to initiate the so-called 'half-price' riots at Drury-Lane, a protest against Garrick's abolition of the half-price entrance fee after the third act of a play, and was thus attacked at greater length by Churchill in additions to *The Rosciad*. See G. W. Stone and G. M. Kahrl, *David Garrick: a Critical Biography* (Carbondale: Southern Illinois University Press, 1979), pp.149-55, for a full account of the controversy.

1032. Sergeant Kite is a character in Vanbrugh's *The Recruiting Officer* (1706), who declares that 'he that has the good fortune to be born six foot high was born to be a great man' (Act I, Scene i, ll. 13-14).

1044. An echo of Pope's *Dunciad*: 'The Monkey-mimicks rush discordant in' (*Dunciad Variorum* (1729), Book 2, 227-8).

1049-54. In the eighteenth century 'Nature' meant, broadly speaking, the natural order and structure of the world.

[From *The Ghost*]
Published in four books. The first two in March 1762, Book 3 in October 1762 and Book 4 in November 1763. Text for Book 3 from the second edition of 1763; for Book 4 from the first edition.

The disparate publication of *The Ghost* spanned most of Churchill's brief poetic career, and as a result the poem has little unity. It shows the influence of Sterne, employing a Shandean ethos of self-justification whenever its digressive nature becomes more than usually apparent. Its title refers to the celebrated contemporary scandal of the 'Cock Lane Ghost'. This involved one William Kent, with his sister-in-law Fanny Lynes a lodger in the house (in Stockwell, in South London) of Richard Parsons in 1759. By Fanny's death in 1760 they had left Parsons' abode; two years later strange knockings were heard in the room of Parsons' eldest daughter, who was soon thought to be acting as a medium for the spirit of Fanny Lynes: from beyond the grave she accused Kent of poisoning her. Many public figures visited the scene of the supposed haunting, which became a sensation. The ingenious accusation of so-called 'scratching Fanny' was subsequently revealed as Parsons' way of framing his former tenant. A committee of investigation (which included Samuel Johnson) concluded that the ghost was a deceit, but the case continued to attract publicity. Kent sought to clear his name by indicting Parsons for conspiring to injure his character. (Churchill witnessed some of the court case; see *Correspondence*, pp.6-7). Parsons was imprisoned for two years, and also had to stand in the pillory three times, where he received much sympathy, and a collection was taken up for him. For a detailed account of the episode, see Douglas Grant, *The Cock Lane Ghost* (London: Macmillan, 1965).

[Book 3, 793-820]
This extract is an attack upon the most significant literary figure of the time, Samuel Johnson (1709-84), called 'Pomposo' by Churchill, a reference to his alleged use of a convoluted style and difficult vocabulary, as well as to his sometimes high-handed public manner. James Gillray's superb print, 'Apollo and the Muses, inflicting Penance on Dr Pomposo,

round Parnassus' (1783), one of the many scathing attacks upon Johnson following the *Lives of the Poets* (1779-81), shows that Churchill's sobriquet held some currency for a time.

The precise reasons for Churchill's dislike of Johnson are unclear, though it seems likely that he was aware of Johnson's opinion of his work. According to Boswell, in 1763, Johnson claimed that '[Churchill] did not attack me violently till he found I did not like his poetry; and his attack on me shall not prevent me from continuing to say what I think of him.' (Boswell, p.297). In the extract, Johnson is one of the three members of a committee set up to ascertain the ghost's existence (the results of which are reprinted by Boswell, pp.288-9, 928).

801-2. Johnson had issued the proposal for his edition of Shakespeare in 1756, when it was promised for completion by the end of 1757. It was not published until 1765.

817-20. Johnson accepted a pension of £300 from George III in 1762. The controversy surrounding this was founded upon the suspicion that Johnson the iconoclast had been paid off, and had become a party hireling. He was often reminded, as by Churchill here, of his previous definition in the *Dictionary* of 'Pension' as 'generally understood as pay given to a state hireling for treason to his country'. It appears that Johnson worried deeply over the implications of his accepting the pension, and consulted friends accordingly (Boswell, pp.264-7). For Churchill, the pension (conferred of course by Bute as Prime Minister) showed Johnson's bad faith and lack of loyalty: 'loves the STUART he forsakes' refers to Johnson's alleged support of the house of Stuart deposed in 1688, and his consequent antipathy towards the Hanoverian monarchy which is now providing him with a pension.

[Book 4, 1685-1910]
The publication of Book 4 of *The Ghost* in November 1763 coincided with the height of John Wilkes's troubles, following his arrest in April for writing number 45 of the *North Briton*. By November, Wilkes's claim that his arrest was a breach of parliamentary privilege was (he thought) soon to be debated in the Commons. Churchill attempted to support his friend,

and thus made the finale of *The Ghost* a mock parade in London on Lord Mayor's day in November 1761, the day after the coronation of George III. Churchill presents the parade as a celebration of the triumph of corruption and anarchy; in this, he is following the description of the 'Great Anarch' that ends Alexander Pope's *Dunciad* (another work that parodies mayoral and royal processions). Yet he also anticipates Percy Bysshe Shelley's *The Mask of Anarchy* (1819), a similarly highly-charged attack upon a government featuring a series of apocalyptic personifications.

1689-90. The '*prison of the North*' is Scotland, with the storms representing Bute's administration, and the increasing Scottish influence in England more generally.

1699. Geryon: in classical mythology, a human monster with three bodies and three heads, who kept flocks of ferocious animals on the island of Gades, in Spain. He was slain by Hercules.

1705-6. The 'Union' is the Act of Union of 1707. Churchill insinuates, typically, that the union with Scotland was greatly to the Scots' benefit, and has encouraged their present gaining of power by underhand means.

1726. The original reads 'Have heads to make or hearts to use', which lacks agreement with the subject of the sentence, and is presumed to be a printer's error.

1729 An echo of the start of Edmund Spenser's *Faerie Queene*: 'And on his brest a bloudie Crosse he bore,/ The deare remembrance of his dying Lord' (Book 1, Canto 1, Stanza 2).

1738-40. The breastplate or 'Rational' (a translation of the Hebrew 'oracular instrument'), made of precious stones, formerly worn by the Jewish high-priest to signify divine instruction and judgment. It is described in Exodus 28: 15-30.

1797-1800. The following long description is of William Murray, First Earl of Mansfield (1705-93), Lord Chief Justice from 1756-88. Churchill's antipathy towards Mansfield stems from his fear of Mansfield's judgment in the impending trial of Wilkes for seditious libel in the Court of King's Bench. Mansfield was considered to take the side of the Crown far too easily in libel prosecutions: 'The defence of a *lawful* excuse never existed in any case before me; therefore I have told the jury that if they were satisfied with the evidence of the publication, and that the meaning of the innuendoes were as stated, they ought to find the defendant guilty' (Mansfield, quoted by W. S. Holdsworth, *A History of English Law*, vol.10 (Methuen, 1938), p.678). Such directions to a jury were vital considerations in Wilkes's case. Mansfield's judgments went against popular feeling in many cases, and he was thus not always a favourite with the public — for example, his house in Bloomsbury Square was looted and burned at one of the worst points of the Gordon riots of 1780, as a result of his support of the Catholic Relief bill.

1811-13. The white rose was the Jacobite emblem; Mansfield's brother was in the service of Charles Edward Stuart, and Mansfield himself was charged with Jacobitism, but exonerated by the cabinet in 1753, though the matter was discussed in the House of Lords (DNB). Churchill plays upon the post-1745 mistrust of those with the vaguest Jacobite potential.

1815-22. Charles Edward Stuart, alias 'Bonnie Prince Charlie', the Young Pretender (1720-88), whose Jacobite uprising of 1745 Churchill is here trying to associate with Mansfield (and, more nebulously, with Scotland generally). 'Nemo me impune lacessit' (touch me not) is the motto of the House of Stuart.

1833-4. The very common allusion is to Prometheus; in one version of the myth, he is chained to a rock by Zeus for having stolen fire to help humanity.

1848. A reference to the allegation that Mansfield had drunk the health of James the Old Pretender at a Jacobite drinking society. See *DNB*, and note to 1811-13.

1853-4. An eloquent, friendly and urbane man, Mansfield is said to have been bullied into some decisions by Sir Fletcher Norton, the aggressive Attorney-General.

1908. Churchill's use of 'or ... or', as opposed to the more modern 'either ... or' is not uncommon in seventeenth and eighteenth century English.

1911-34. This somewhat anti-climatic and confusing conclusion can be explained by Churchill's need to distance himself, legally, from the virulent preceding description. Thus he names Mansfield as an innocent force of justice who has come from Scotland to liberate Britain from the tyrannical figure just described. That this tyrannical figure represented Churchill's real opinion of Mansfield is beyond doubt.

The Prophecy of Famine. A Scots Pastoral

Published in January 1763. Text from fifth edition (also 1763). Churchill included earlier passages of the poem in letters to Wilkes of 1762, where it was first referred to as the 'Scottish Eclogue' (*Correspondence*, pp.21, 24-7). It was evidently designed as a piece of anti-Bute propaganda, along the lines of other parodies of Scottishness in the *North Briton*. Churchill's use of mock-pastoral, with its images of poverty, starvation, disease and relentless acquisitiveness, was typical of anti-Scottish prejudice of the time (as discussed in the Introduction). The frontispiece to the original quarto edition of the poem is a hideous engraving of 'Famine' outside her cave. The vigour of Churchill's invective won the admiration of the Scot James Boswell (Boswell, p.297), but otherwise attracted much hostility: the poem found an angry response from the poet John Langhorne, who riposted with *Genius and Valour: A Pastoral Poem, Written in Honour of a Sister Kingdom* (1764), a work that attempted to reverse Churchill's slurs by pointing out as many favourable things about Scotland as possible. (Langhorne might have been motivated by his friendship for Lord Lyttelton and other poets satirised by Churchill; see Grant, p.543). Churchill undoubtedly produced the more powerful poem, for all its wild prejudice.

The poem's epigraph is taken from an oration on the installation of the Jacobite Earl of Westmoreland by Dr William King (1685-1763), at Oxford University in 1759. King, a notorious Jacobite, is quoting the concluding line of Virgil's ninth Eclogue, which translates 'Our songs we shall sing the better, when the master himself is come' (translated by H. Rushton Fairclough (London: Loeb, 1924), p.74). The 'master' is an obvious reference to the Pretender, and commences Churchill's linking of the Scottish with Jacobitism, a connection upon which the poem is structured.

9. Mount Parnassus, home of the Muses.

17. 'LARDELLA' – a name in obvious mockery of the tradition of pastoral romance.
18. Echoing Pope's *Essay on Man*, 1,140: 'My foot-stool earth, my canopy the skies'.
27. Zephyr is the west wind.
29-45. A reference to Bute's artistic patronage, which Churchill always assumed to be motivated by his desire for political propaganda, or Scottish cronyism.
47. Theocritus, the Greek poet most associated with the development of pastoral as a poetic genre.
48. Virgil (Publius Vergilius Maro), the great Roman poet, was born on the banks of the river Mincius.
51-8. Churchill is mocking the then current trend for poetry of affected sentiment and heightened sensibility.
63-66. Churchill's insult is reminiscent of Alexander Pope's put-down of Richard Bentley and Lewis Theobald, emendatory or 'textual' critics, in the *Epistle to Dr. Arbuthnot:* 'The things, we know, are neither rich nor rare,/ But wonder how the Devil they got there?' (171-172).
67. William Mason (1724-97), remembered now mainly as the friend and executor of Thomas Gray, was a poet much ridiculed for the lofty affectation and sentimentality of his verses. His *Musæus: A Monody to the Memory of Mr. Pope, in Imitation of Milton's Lycidas* (1747), exhibits precisely the extravagant sort of poetic sensibility that Churchill is attacking.
69. The architect William Chambers had erected a so-called 'Great Pagoda' in the garden at Kew, home of the Dowager Princess of Wales; she was reputed by much gossip to have been the Earl of Bute's lover, hence the popular title of the Pagoda as 'Bute's Erection'. See Hamilton, p.39.
70. The Princess Dowager's alleged affair with Bute was the subject of and motivation behind *Gisbal: an Hyperborean Tale* (1762), a work satirising Bute's administration, and the Ossianic works of James Macpherson.
71-2. Lord Lyttelton (1709-73) had by 1756 fallen out with the administration of Churchill's hero William Pitt, hence his inclusion here; he was also a friend and patron to many writers, including the Scotsmen James Thomson and (more pertinently, for Churchill) Bute's particular

supporter David Mallet. Churchill's comment on his '*faith*' refers to his *Observations on the Conversion and Apostleship of St Paul* (1747), praised for its devotion and wisdom by Samuel Johnson.

74-6. A reference to Lyttelton's *To the Memory of a Lady Lately Deceased, a Monody* (1747), a poem concerning the death of his first wife, Lucy Fortescue.

77. Presumably a reference to Lyttelton's patronage of Scottish writers like Thomson (cf. William Collins's ode on Thomson's death (1749), with its famous opening, 'In yonder grave a Druid lies').

78. Editions of Lyttelton's last work, a *History of Henry the Second*, were inexplicably reprinted four times in his lifetime, from 1755-71, as a result of an expensive (and ultimately futile) search for accuracy. See Samuel Johnson, *Lives of the Poets*, ed. G. Birkbeck Hill, 3 vols (Oxford: Clarendon, 1905), 3, pp.453-4.

79-92. A typical example of Churchill's carefully crafted apologies for his own lack of poetic craft and skill, as well as an attack on excessive poetic sensibility.

85. Mason's poetry was notoriously alliterative.

93. More self-mockery, quoting Edmund's famous declaration (*King Lear*, I, ii, 1).

94. 'Hence' here and at line 97 is dismissive, meaning 'away', rather than 'consequently'.

107-10. Churchill's turns towards northern climes are invariably ironic; the '*loyal Laird*' and '*faithful clan*' are obvious references to the Jacobite uprising of 1745.

116. That Bute's family name was the (hardly uncommon) 'Stuart' was latched upon by opposition writers invoking, as Churchill does here, the latent threat of the exiled Stuart monarchy.

121-2. A reference to the Scots' allegedly perfidious treatment of Charles I. Having surrendered to the Scottish in 1646, he was handed over to the Parliamentary army in 1647, after a financial agreement had been struck.

123. In the eighteenth century, 'science' meant intellectual learning or knowledge, in a far less specific sense than its present meaning.

125-6. Allan Ramsay the elder (1686-1758), Scottish poet and author of

The Gentle Shepherd: A Scots Pastoral (1725), a drama parodied later in the poem by Churchill. His son, Allan Ramsay (1713-84) had become painter to George III in 1761, and enjoyed Bute's patronage. He was supposed to have Jacobite sympathies, though his modern biographer points out the absurdity of this, as Ramsay had written an anti-Jacobite poem in 1745. See Alastair Smart, *The Life and Art of Allan Ramsay* (London: Routledge, 1952), pp.102-4.

128. Despite his status as a Church minister, John Home (1722-1808) created something of a scandal with the production of his play *Douglas* in 1756. After resigning from his ministry Home moved to London; he benefited from Bute's patronage, and was awarded a £300 annual pension, as well as a salaried position. See Richard B. Sher, 'The Favourite of the Favourite', in *Lord Bute: Essays in Reinterpretation*, ed. Karl W. Schweizer (Leicester: Leicester University Press, 1988), 181-212, for a discussion of Home's close friendship with Bute.

129. Churchill uses Home's example to complain of his own treatment by the 'Dull Dean' of Westminster, Zachary Pearce, who had reprimanded him for his manner of dress and general behaviour in 1762, thus precipitating his resignation from the Church in January 1763, the time of the poem's publication. (See Brown, pp.84-6.)

129-30. James Macpherson (1736-96) initiated one of the most notorious cultural arguments of the century with the publication of *Fragments of Ancient Poetry* (1761), the first of the series of fragments supposedly translated from Gaelic that would also include *Fingal* (1762) and *Temora* (1763). The controversy behind the authenticity of the poems was jumped upon gleefully by Churchill, as 'Ossian', the supposed author, was an emblem of Scottish nationalism, and the 'Advertisement' to *Fingal* had ended with fulsome praise for Bute.

131-4. Praising Bute was also an occupation of David Malloch (1705?-65), subsequently Mallet, poet and playwright, who had done his best for the Earl in dedicating his tragedy *Elvira* (first produced at Drury Lane on 19 January 1763) to him. Bute rewarded Mallet with the job of Keeper of the Books of the Port of London. Mallet's former notoriety was as the posthumous editor of Bolingbroke's allegedly atheistic and impious

philosophical works in 1754, hence Churchill's sneering remark on the 'rewards' of *daring infidels*.
145. See 2 Kings 5:10-14, for the story of the healing of Namaan the leper.
159-62. Wilkes had visited Scotland in 1758 (as he mentions during his famous meeting with Johnson). See Boswell, p.771.
189. Moses viewed the promised land from Pisgah (Deuteronomy 3:27).
211-12. St Paul's phrase, 'I am made all things to all men' (1 Corinthians 9:22).
217-22. A mock-apology for his anti-Scottish invective in the *North Briton*.
222. This suggests that Churchill's mother was Scottish; there is no other information about her.
232. Gilbert West (1703-56) poet and author of *Observations on the History and Evidence of the Resurrection* (1747), a work said to have inspired his friend, Lyttelton's previously mentioned treatise on St Paul (see Johnson, *Lives of the Poets*, 3, pp.329-30). The two tracts were often reprinted in the same volume, and referred to by the two surnames, as here.
242. The 'Thane' is Bute.
245-6. John Hill (1716-75), was formerly a dramatist, before his farce *The Rout* failed in 1758. Under the patronage of Bute he produced many scientific writings and tracts, with botany a particular concern.
250. For John Home, see 128.
255-8. William Whitehead (1715-85), Poet Laureate since 1757. His *A Charge to the Poets* (1762) criticised contemporary poetic invective in lines which clearly had the *Rosciad* in mind (See Grant, pp.492-3).
269-70. Another swipe at the authenticity of 'Ossian', with a pun on 'simplicity' also.
272. Another allusion to Johnson's description of 'pension' as pay for a 'state hireling' in his *Dictionary*. See note to *The Ghost*, 4, 817-20.
281. 'Jockey' and 'Sawney' were the most common contemptuous names for the Scottish in the eighteenth century: 'Sawney' in particular seems to have first been used at the beginning of the century (OED); 'Sawney Gesner' was one of Bute's insulting nicknames.
290. For John Home see 128; for *Fingal* see 129-30.

293. As discussed in the Introduction, images of the Scottish as diseased and lice-ridden are a constant in anti-Butean literature and prints of the period. Wilkes and his friend Thomas Potter even lampooned the hygiene of Scottish women in one of the facetious footnotes to their *Essay on Woman* (see Hamilton, p.229).

307-8. The 10th of June, the Young Pretender's birthday, brought forth the white rose, the Jacobite emblem.

311-34. The description of the Cave of Famine owes something to the Cave of Spleen in Pope's *The Rape of the Lock* (Canto 4, 16-36).

329. An eft is a small lizard, akin to a newt.

335-402. The description and the following dialogue between Jockey and Sawney parodies the conversation between Patie and Roger, in the opening of Allan Ramsay's drama *The Gentle Shepherd* (1725), Act I, Scene i, 1-170.

345. An echo of Lear in the storm (*King Lear* III, iv, 28-9).

369-70. The sentiment is, appropriately, an echo of John Langhorne's poetic version of the book of Job (1760): 'Didst thou exist before the Lamp of Day?/ Or whence proceeds thy boasted Wisdom, say?' (*Job, a Poem*, Book 3, 191-2).

375. The tobacco plant, presumably.

381-6. The 'year' is 1745, and the Jacobite rebellion: the Young Pretender 'discreetly fled' to the continent upon its failure in 1746, and severe reprisals against his followers subsequently took place in the Highlands.

397. A 'Ferrara' was another name for the claymore, or highland broadsword (after Andrea Ferrara, the name of a famous maker of swords in Ferrara in Italy).

402. A reference to the earlier Jacobite uprising of 1715.

421-2. A parody of the divine intervention common in Classical epic.

441-2. See note to ll.121-2.

447-450. An allusion to Moses being told of the deliverance of the people of Israel from Egypt. See Exodus 3:8.

469-72. Churchill may have in mind the conclusion of Pope's *Windsor Forest* (1713), and its vision of Britain's trees becoming ships and travelling the world in the service of the nation's commerce (385-400).

477-486. A reference to Bute's most significant political move – the unpopular Peace of the Treaty of Paris (the Preliminaries of which had been passed through Parliament in December 1762), which brought the end of the Seven Years War.

505-10. Although the allusion is suitably vague, the subject here could the abortive Jacobite uprising of 1715, when the Earl of Mar (a Secretary of State under Queen Anne) led the army of James the Pretender in Scotland, before retreating to France in 1716 once the attempt had failed.

511-16. The historical subject of this passage is ambivalent. I believe it to be a reference to the War of the Austrian Succession, which saw most of the British army fighting the French in the Netherlands in June 1745, when the Jacobite uprising began, hence the 'weak land'. Tooke (1, p.206) thinks it refers to the invasion of northern England by the Scots in 1346, which took place whilst Edward III was fighting in France.

529. The King James Bible's rendering of St Paul (I Corinthians 13:2).

530-3 Bute is Famine's 'son' with the royal name of Stuart.

535. Luke 3:5.

540. A reference to William Pitt the Elder, and his resignation in 1761.

545. A reference to the Treaty of Paris.

553-6. Either a reference to William III, saviour in Whig popular history of the country from the Stuart monarchy in 1688, or a more immediate allusion to William, Duke of Cumberland (1721-65), son of George II, victor of Culloden, the chief impetus behind the quelling of the 1745 uprising, and a useful symbol of anti-Scottishness for Churchill, especially as he opposed Bute's planned Peace.

An Epistle to William Hogarth

Published in June 1763; text from first edition.

The epigraph is one of the most quoted parts of Horace's *Ars Poetica*, and translates 'as with the painter's work, so with the poet.' The concept of 'ut pictura poesis', and the relationship between poetry and painting, was a key subject of eighteenth-century aesthetics.

Churchill's poem springs from a sequence of events that begin in 1762, when William Hogarth (1697-1764), the most significant British painter and engraver of the first half of the century, planned a print called *The*

Times, which would be in favour of Bute's plans for peace, and a satire on Pitt and the opposition. Hogarth had previously been on good (or at least neutral) terms with Wilkes and Churchill, and was not renowned for giving direct political support through his work. Wilkes, on hearing of his plan, warned him of retaliation; Hogarth appears to have ignored the warning, telling Wilkes that neither he nor Churchill would be directly portrayed. When the print appeared in September, it was clear that the two figures spraying water from a garret upon Bute (as he tries to put out the fires of war and faction) would have been identified as Wilkes and Churchill by anyone with the ability to read a satirical print.

Wilkes's response was swift and telling: the *North Briton* No.17 (25 September 1762) was a character assassination of Hogarth. Hogarth's revenge came when he viewed Wilkes at the Court of Common Pleas on 6 May 1763, arguing that his imprisonment was a breach of his parliamentary privilege. On 21 May, Hogarth produced a devastating caricature of a malevolent, grinning Wilkes holding a staff on top of which is the cap of Liberty. Churchill had been meditating an attack upon Hogarth for some time (see *Correspondence*, pp. 48, 52-5), and was stung into action. After the poem's publication, Hogarth caricatured him in the print 'The Bruiser' (August 1763), which depicted Churchill as a giant bear wielding a club littered with various 'lies'.

The best account of the context of the poem is Ronald Paulson's *Hogarth, His Life, Art and Times: Volume 3, Art and Politics, 1750-1764* (Cambridge: Lutterworth Press, 1993), pp.362-412. Paulson makes the telling point that Wilkes and Hogarth were appealing to the same area of society in their satiric works, thus making their dispute even less necessary. Hogarth worked on an unfinished sequel, *The Times* plate II, which confounded all factions, mocking Bute as much as Pitt or Wilkes. The story, common in the nineteenth century, that the attacks upon Hogarth by Wilkes and Churchill caused his death, is without foundation: he was far from well before the controversy, and his eventual death in October 1764 (nine days before that of Churchill) owed nothing to its effects, which were hardly long-lasting.

22. Henry Fox (1705-74) later Lord Holland. Paymaster-General, made

leader of the House of Commons in 1762 by Bute, who gained a politician with an underhand reputation to help pass the Preliminaries of the Treaty of Paris through Parliament. Fox gained a peerage from Bute for his services, which were thought to consist essentially of bribing the Commons: 'and with so little decorum on the part of buyer or seller, that a shop was publicly opened at the Pay Office, wither the members flocked, and received the wages of their venality in bank-bills' (Walpole, 1, pp.156-7). It should be added that some modern historians have rejected these accusations: see Langford, pp.350-1, and Louis Namier, *The Structure of Politics at the Accession of George III*, 2nd edn (London: Macmillan, 1961), pp.181-4. After the passing of the Preliminaries, Fox went on the offensive against those who had voted against them (see Walpole, 1, pp.184-9). Always associated with political corruption, Fox was also the target of Thomas Gray's superb satire 'On Lord Holland's Seat Near Margate', concerning his fashionably ruined home at Kingsgate.

Sir Francis Dashwood (1708-81), founded the notorious Hell Fire Club at Medmenhem Abbey in Marlow, which both Churchill and Wilkes had attended. His being made Chancellor of the Exchequer in 1762 brought forth much wry amusement from those aware of his lack of intellectual prowess. As Wilkes put it, 'From puzzling all his life at tavern bills, he was called by Lord Bute to administer the finances of a kingdom above one hundred million in debt' (see Hamilton, p.71). Dashwood's own estimate of his abilities was not high: Walpole reports him saying 'People will point at me and cry, *There goes the worst Chancellor of the Exchequer that ever appeared*', after his Budget speech of 1763, which was, in Walpole's words, 'of little intelligence or clearness' (Walpole, 1, p.198).

55. Grant (p.476), sees that Churchill's use of 'candour' is now obsolete. Rather than the modern sense of 'honesty', he means by it 'freedom from malice, favourable disposition, kindliness' (OED 4). St Paul extols charity in 1 Corinthians 13.

57. Lady Macbeth's famous judgment on her husband's nature: 'It is too full o' th' milk of human kindness' (I, v, 17).

63. From John Dryden's *MacFlecknoe*: 'And torture one poor word ten thousand ways' (208).

75. Sir Fletcher Norton (1716-89) was made Attorney-General in 1763, and was directly concerned with the prosecution of Wilkes for the alleged seditious libel in No.45 of *The North Briton*. Norton's aggressive conduct was to have considerable bearing on Wilkes's case. An obstreperous and difficult man, according to Walpole, Norton took bribes to decide cases as a matter of course (Walpole, 1, pp.189-90).

76. For Mansfield, see note to *The Ghost*, 4, 1797-1800.

82. A reference to Wilkes's arrest on a general warrant on 30 April 1763. Grant (p.520), glosses Churchill's legal subtlety in the line very clearly: 'the warrant of commitment required the Constable to receive him into custody "for being the author and publisher of a most infamous and seditious libel." Thus it was "prejudged" that Wilkes was guilty before he had stood trial'.

83-4. Wilkes was discharged on 6 May 1763 in the Court of Common Pleas by Chief Justice Pratt. It was on this occasion that Hogarth sketched what would become his caricature of Wilkes (See Thomas, pp.30-31, Hamilton, pp.73-4).

110. Churchill's resignation from the Church in January 1763.

115. 'Lawn' is the name of the fine linen used for the sleeves of a bishop; hence 'lawn' is a metonym for 'the dignity or office of a bishop' (OED, where Churchill is cited).

116. Zachary Pearce, Bishop of Rochester, Churchill's ecclesiastical bête noire. See note on *The Prophecy of Famine*, 129.

126-130. The OED defines 'Prudence' primarily as the 'Ability to discern the most suitable, politic, or profitable course of action, esp. as regards conduct: practical wisdom, discretion.' The potential conflict between the most politic and the most profitable course of action is exploited by Churchill repeatedly in his poetry, where 'Prudence' always carries an undertone of duplicity.

137-8. See Grant, p.520, for the claim that Churchill had advertised an intended satire on women.

140. John Ayliffe, steward to Henry Fox, was executed in 1759 for forging Fox's name on a lease of an estate to himself. Tooke (1, pp.227-8) claims that Ayliffe expected a pardon, in return for his silence (presumably

through the influence of Fox). Churchill advertised a poem called 'Ayliffe's Ghost', which was never written. According to Wilkes, Fox's emissary tried to bribe Churchill into not writing the poem, but was rebuffed (see Brown, pp.103-4).

141-6. The reference is to Pope's famous attack on Joseph Addison in *An Epistle to Dr Arbuthnot*, 193-214.

160. An echo of much-imitated lines in Thomas Gray's *Elegy Written in a Country Churchyard*: 'Full many a flower is born to blush unseen,/ And waste its sweetness on the desert air' (55-6).

165. 'Puling' – crying or whimpering.

183-224. The passage bears some resemblance to the conclusion of Pope's *Epilogue to the Satires*, Dialogue I (137-72), and the triumph of 'Vice' described there.

184. The promotion of the piety of George III's Court was used by the opposition as another example of Bute's disingenuousness, given the behaviour of most of its leading lights, and its political scandals.

185-6. A Bill was put forward by the ill-starred Chancellor, Sir Francis Dashwood, to tax cider and perry, in March 1763. The cider tax was deeply unpopular and ill-timed, giving more ammunition to those criticising the administration (particularly as it extended the powers of excise officers greatly), and was a factor in precipitating Bute's resignation on 8 April.

187-8. Churchill's attitude towards homosexuality is not one of his more endearing or enlightened facets; he would later rail against it at tedious length in his Juvenalian satire *The Times* (1764).

195-6. A reference to Lord Edward Wortley Montagu (1681-1761) husband of the writer Lady Mary. He left his huge fortune to his daughter Mary, rather than to his son Edward, a very eccentric and debt-ridden traveller and writer who had earned his father's displeasure for an ill-advised marriage, and much other peculiar behaviour. Edward planned to dispute the Will, which made the case public knowledge. His sister Mary was the Earl of Bute's wife, hence Churchill's condemnation. See Isobel Grundy, *Lady Mary Wortley Montagu: Comet of the Enlightenment* (Oxford: Oxford University Press, 1999), pp.601-7, and elsewhere, for Edward's disaster-prone career.

199. Samuel Martin, MP, Joint Secretary to the Treasury. See headnote to *The Duellist*.

200. Philip Carteret Webb (1700-70), Joint Solicitor to the Treasury. On the arrest of Wilkes in April, Webb was supervisor (with Robert Wood (1717-71), the Under-Secretary of State), of the seizure of Wilkes's papers and the search of his house. Wilkes brought actions against Wood and Webb for illegal arrest; Webb was found not guilty of perjury in evidence given at Wood's trial, and was not tried himself before his own demise. Tooke (1, pp.230-3) details his vast antiquarian learning and possessions, and dismisses Walpole's low opinion of him. To the latter, Webb was 'a most villainous tool and agent in any iniquity' (Walpole, 1, p.219).

202. A reference to Henry Fox's being made Lord Holland, in April 1763, as a reward for services to Bute (see note to 22).

205-8. John Calcraft (1716-92), Henry Fox's nephew, reputed to be his son. Fox's peerage was made conditional to his quitting the role of Paymaster-General. He at first refused, and Calcraft sided with Lord Shelburne against his putative father, despite his having made, as an army agent, enormous amounts of money from Fox's influence. See Lord Ilchester, *Henry Fox, Lord Holland*, 2 vols. (London: John Murray, 1920), 2, pp.238-261.

208. Bute's resignation on 8 April was greeted by a common fear that he continued to rule the administration and monarch in all but name. Walpole claimed to have seen Bute write that '*whatever the ministers might think, they should find he himself was minister still*. A memorable assertion, confirmed by facts, and of which the contrary assertion was vainly attempted afterwards to be imposed upon the world' (Walpole, 1, p.237).

Grant (p.522) sees a reference here to rumours of the demise of Lord Holland, following his departure for the continent after April 1763 (see Ilchester, *Henry Fox, Lord Holland*, 2, p.263).

211-12. Possibly an echo of Pope's apologia for the satirist and poet in the *Epistle to Dr Arbuthnot*: 'That not in Fancy's Maze he wander'd long,/ But stoop'd to Truth, and moraliz'd his song' (340-1).

225-7. A reference to *The Rosciad*.

228. Churchill's second poem, *The Apology. Addressed to the Critical Reviewers* (1761), a response to reviews of *The Rosciad*.
229-230. A more general allusion, probably to *The Prophecy of Famine*.
244. An echo of *Hamlet*, where 'the native hue of resolution/ Is sicklied, o'er with the pale cast of thought' (III, i, 84-5).
329-40. The main focus of Churchill's attack upon Hogarth, his envy at the achievements of other artists, is an exaggeration, though it plays upon well-known elements of Hogarth's character, especially his pride. His related charge, that Hogarth enviously hampered the careers of promising painters, is equally without foundation, though Hogarth could be very mordant about artists and the state of art. See Jenny Uglow, *Hogarth* (London: Faber & Faber, 1994), pp.570-5, for one such example. Churchill follows Wilkes's attack on Hogarth in *North Briton* No.17, which had also accused him of vanity, and of denigrating famous predecessors.
368. An echo of Dryden's 'The Twenty Ninth Ode of the Third Book of Horace', where the 'tide of business' is 'always in extreme' (55).
389-92. A reference to Hogarth's print, *The Times*.
401-2. The Magna Carta, symbol of English liberty since its being obtained from King John in 1215.
403-8. Churchill's rather melodramatic description of Wilkes's brief imprisonment. See note to 83-4.
409-12. See note to 83-4.
480-6. Churchill's new subject is far closer to Hogarth's heart, being perhaps the biggest disappointment of his career. At a sale in 1758, a painting of 'Sigismunda weeping over the Heart of Guiscardo' (mistakenly attributed to Corregio) sold for £404 5s. It would seem that this encouraged Hogarth's latent desire to be respected in the same genre of history painting, and he set out to paint on the same tragic subject (in a story from Bocaccio's *Decameron*, Sigismunda's lover is murdered by her jealous father, and she receives his heart in a goblet). He accepted an apparently open commission from Sir Richard Grosvenor for £400. However, Grosvenor refused the finished painting in June 1759. Hogarth refused to lower the value of the painting. He exhibited it in 1761, and also tried to raise a subscription for an engraving of it. Both were

unsuccessful. It was eventually sold posthumously, in 1790, for only £58 16s. 'Sigismunda' thus became something of a millstone in Hogarth's declining years. Wilkes had already criticised it in *North Briton* No.17. See Paulson, *Hogarth, His Life, Art and Times:* Volume 3, pp.223-33, 322-5, 429. 488-90. John Dryden's verse translation of 'Sigismunda and Guiscardo' is one of the most striking of his *Fables, Ancient and Modern* (1700).

493-500. As well as changing Guiscardo from Sigismunda's lover to her husband, Dryden makes Sigismunda a figure of great dignity and sympathy, giving her a powerful speech in defence of female freedom which Tancred, her tyrannical father, cannot answer. Hogarth's 'Sigismunda', Churchill argues (not entirely unfairly), falls a long way short in comparison.

501. Echoing Satan's first speech to Beelzebub in *Paradise Lost:* 'If thou beest he; but oh how fallen! how changed' (Book 1, 84).

508. Grant (p.523), takes this to refer to Bonnell Thornton's Sign Painters' exhibition of 1762, where a portrait of 'Hogarth's head' is listed. It may also be a more general insult, implying that Hogarth's style of painting is akin to (and an influence for) sign painting, and thus crude and limited. Hogarth was apparently involved in the exhibition (see Paulson, *Hogarth, His Life, Art and Times*: Volume 3, pp.351-61).

517. Hogarth was Serjeant Painter to the King, a job lampooned by his enemies as that of a mere tradesman. Wilkes called him a 'pannel-painter' (*North Briton*, No.17, 25 September 1762).

518. The downfall of Pitt the Elder and Earl Temple in 1761, which ushered in Bute's ministry. See Introduction.

519-22. After the Peace had been signed at the Treaty of Paris in March, congratulatory addresses to the King were sought by the administration, but relatively few were forthcoming (see Walpole, 1, pp.222-3).

528. Amongst the opposition, the Treaty was heavily criticised for conceding all the ground gained commercially during the Seven Years War. See Langford (pp.350-351) for a list of gains and losses, and a questioning of the 'supposed unpopularity of the Peace.' Reasons for such unpopularity are discussed in Steven Watson's *The Reign of George III* (Oxford: Clarendon Press, 1960), pp.84-88.

576. In this context, '*Sublime*' as a style, indicates the sort of painting (of mythology or history) capable of gaining an exalted and extended emotional response.

599-600. Savage giants people the way towards Canaan (Deuteronomy 2-3).

634. Jonathan Swift's mental and physical faculties were severely impaired for at least three years before his death in 1745; he had already been used in Samuel Johnson's *The Vanity of Human Wishes* as a similar example of greatness decayed, where he 'expires a driveller and a show' (318). The essayist and dramatist Sir Richard Steele (1672-1729), was partially paralysed by a stroke for the last three years of his life.

654. Sir Joshua Reynolds (1723-92) avoided such a fate. The dominant English portrait painter of the time, the first President of the Royal Academy and an important aesthetician in his *Discourses* (1769-90), Reynolds aligned English painting further with the European tradition, and was a figure of considerable cultural influence.

[From *The Duellist*]
First published in January 1764. Text from second edition.

The simultaneous attack on Wilkes for the *North Briton* No.45 and *An Essay on Woman* in the House of Lords and the Commons on 15 November 1763 was also an excuse for Samuel Martin MP (previously criticised in the *North Briton* Nos. 37 and 40 for his help in bribing the Treaty of Paris through Parliament) to take his revenge upon Wilkes. During the debate preceding voting the *North Briton* No.45 a seditious libel, Martin 'had risen and called the author of "that paper" a cowardly, scandalous, and malignant scoundrel"' (Walpole, 1, p.252). Wilkes wrote to him the next day, claiming responsibility, and Martin having issued a challenge, the two fought a duel at midday in Hyde Park. Both missed, but Martin hit Wilkes in the side the second time, and fled, at Wilkes entreaty, to escape prosecution.

Martin's actions appeared premeditated: 'It was thought an ill symptom of Martin's courage that he had smothered the affront for so many months'. Furthermore, he had been observed practising his marksmanship all summer (Walpole, 1, pp.252-3). He became ironically known as 'Target' Martin (*St James's Chronicle*, 22 November 1763). The case therefore became, for Churchill and others, a plot to assassinate Wilkes. *The Duellist* is Churchill's poetic account of this conspiracy. As well as Martin, it targets the Fourth Earl of Sandwich (1718-92), Wilkes's former associate in the Hell Fire Club, who was ridiculed for his reading from *An Essay on Woman* in the Lords and pretending to be scandalised at its obscenities, given his own notorious behaviour. Churchill's other conspirator, William Warburton, Bishop of Gloucester, was the pretended author of the footnotes to the poem. His anger in the Lords helped to get the poem voted a blasphemy and a breach of privilege against his person; for Churchill's longer retaliation against Warburton, see the 'Dedication to the Sermons'. The extract here illustrates something of the flavour of Churchill's use of the octosyllabic couplet, a form with the momentum to support his praise of English 'liberty', the keystone of Wilkes's campaign.

167. John Hampden (1594-1643), refused to pay the widely disliked 'Ship Money' to Charles I in 1635, and was an influential parliamentary figure (not least as one of the five MPs that Charles tried to arrest in January 1642, a major incident on the road to Civil War). He became a symbolic figure for those with republican sympathies, or for Whiggish writers defending the idea of liberty more generally.

169-70. Algernon Sidney (1622-83), another republican and Whig hero, prime mover with William, Lord Russell behind the Rye House Plot of 1683, an unsuccessful plan to assassinate Charles II and his brother James at Newmarket, Suffolk, which cost Sidney his life.

200. 'Lethe' – the river of the underworld which made its denizens forget the past.

248. For Samuel Martin, see headnote.

[From *Gotham*]
The three books of the poem were published in February, March and October 1764.

Churchill's most unusual work, *Gotham* takes as its starting point the idea of the poet as monarch of the island of the 'Gothamites' (the inhabitants of Gotham, a village in Nottinghamshire, had long been proverbial for their foolishness). This would appear to be yet another way of satirising Bute and George III. However, although the poem does contain some lampooning of George as a 'Patriot King' (an important political idea promoted by the Tory thinker Henry St John Bolingbroke in the 1730s), the poem is by turns a description of Churchill's Utopia, a discussion of poetic and creative genius, a Whig panegyric, and a debate on the limits of abstract reasoning when applied to the *realpolitik* of government. From this range of subjects, the extract (the opening of Book 1), illustrates another unusual side of Churchill's writing – a critique of the ideology of Empire and the sufferings of native peoples under colonialism.

3. Sir John Mandeville was thought to be the author of a well-known book of travels, published (in French) in 1356-7. Mandeville's supposed 'travels' in the East were a compilation of older sources, under the aegis of a spurious travel narrative: they have become celebrated for their fantastical and absurd marvels.

25. 'Half the Ball' – half the globe.

49. The usual reference to the Magna Carta as the bulwark of English liberty.

72. After an act of 1717, first-time offenders could be transported to America for a term of seven years, and those on capital sentences could be sent for fourteen: 'While occasional convicts had been sent over since the time of the Restoration, the numbers now greatly increased, reaching a total of thirty thousand by 1760'. See Richard Middleton, *Colonial America: a History, 1607-1760* (Oxford: Blackwell, 1992), pp.189-90.

87. The powerful religious sect of the Pharisees are repeatedly accused in the Gospels of misrepresenting the word of God for their own, secular means.

95-8. Although the English had been involved in India in the seventeenth century, the mid-eighteenth century saw the East India Company consolidate its position there. For Churchill's more specific attack on the

Company and Robert Clive, its most significant figure, see *The Farewell*, 453-91, and notes.
120. A 'punctilio' is a trifling or minor point concerning behaviour or etiquette.
127-8. The walls of the city of Thebes were supposed to have been built by the sound of Amphion's lyre.
131-2. According to Grant (p.535), Monmouth Street in Seven Dials, London, was well-known for selling old clothes. He cites Brewer's *Dictionary of Phrase and Fable*: 'hence the expression *Monmouth Street finery* for tawdry, pretentious clothes'.
144. The parish of St Giles in the Fields, between Covent Garden and Oxford Street, infamous for crime, squalor, and disease: 'It was an area linked with rookeries and thieves' dens, around the crowded labyrinth of Seven Dials' (Pat Rogers, *Hacks and Dunces* (London: Methuen, 1980), p.73).
144-6. Churchill was born in Vine Street in Westminster. See Grant, p.535, and Brown, p.218, n.22, for the claim that Churchill offended his aunt and lost a legacy with these lines (a story which sounds fanciful, and which is now unverifiable).
147. Bonnell Thornton (1724-68), Churchill's friend and former schoolfellow at Westminster. The reference is to his *An Ode on St Cecilia's Day* (June 1763), a burlesque of the tradition of songs to the Saint of music, such as Dryden's 'Song to St Cecilia's Day' (1687), and 'Alexander's Feast' (1697).
158. William Boyce (1710-79), Master of the King's Music (the band of musicians who accompanied the monarch, and played at ceremonial events) since 1755.
165-236. Although he does not adhere to it particularly closely (except for the odd phrase), Churchill's model for his description of the five ages of man is Jacques' famous speech on the seven ages of man in *As You Like It* (II,vii, 143-66).
184. The child's spinning-top.
207. An echo of the first appearance of Adam and Eve in *Paradise Lost:* 'for in their looks divine/ The image of their glorious maker shone' (Book

4, 291-2).
215-34. Churchill perhaps draws upon the spirit of Samuel Johnson's portrait of an old, covetous 'dotard' in *The Vanity of Human Wishes*, 255-290.

The Farewell

Published in June 1764. Text from first edition.

In 1763, Wilkes had urged Churchill to address government interference in the East India Company in the *North Briton* (see *Correspondence*, pp.50-2). Accordingly, he wrote a rather dry issue on the subject, which was not printed because of Bute's resignation and the ensuing furore over *North Briton* No.45. The struggle for power within the East India Company had become a matter of public interest by 1764. In this struggle, Wilkes supported Robert Clive (1725-74), the most controversial figure in the development of British India in the century. Clive's argument with the Directors of the Company is described below. What is interesting is that Churchill does not absolve Clive from his satire: the end of the poem places him as part of the ongoing process of British exploitation of India, with the prophetic suggestion that there are more future scandals waiting to be revealed. The poem is one of Churchill's more Popean works, adopting the structure of a dialogue between the poet (marked 'P'), and his unnamed friend ('F'). In this, and in its argument of the necessity of satire in times so ridden with public iniquity, it follows the two dialogues that make up Pope's *Epilogue to the Satires* (1738).

10. Sirius the Dog-star appears in late Summer, and is thus associated with heady temperatures and extreme mental states. Churchill undoubtedly alludes to the opening of Pope's *Epistle to Dr Arbuthnot:* 'The Dog-star rages! Nay 'tis past a doubt,/ All Bedlam, or Parnassus, is let out' (3-4).
27-8. A phrase that has become a commonplace. A possible influence on Churchill's schoolfriend William Cowper who, in 'The Timepiece', the second book of *The Task* (1785), declared that 'England with all thy faults, I love thee still' (206).

46. The advice to beware that you do not lose the substance by grasping at shadows originates in Aesop's fable of 'The Dog and the Meat', sometimes called 'The Dog and the Shadow', *Aesop's Fables*, ed. Samuel Richardson (London, 1740), p.4. Churchill uses the metaphor again in the 'Dedication to the Sermons', 157.

51. A reference to the 'Schoolmen' or 'Scholiasts', medieval thinkers who synthesised the writings of the Church Fathers with the philosophical ideas of Aristotle. They were often referred to in a pejorative sense as an example of arid, dogmatic and over-literal thinking.

105-6. Diogenes of Sinope (413-324 BC), a famous Cynic philosopher, renowned for his disdain for worldly vanity and the luxury of all possessions, who generated many probably apocryphal stories. Churchill's reference is to the story that 'Diogenes trod under foot *Plato's* robe, saying I tread underfoot *Plato's* pride: But, *Diogenes*, answer'd *Plato*, how proud are you yourself, when you think you contemn pride?' Thomas Stanley, *The History of Philosophy*, 2 vols (London:, 1656), 2, Part 7, p.16. As Tooke points out (3, p.194), Diogenes proclaimed himself 'a citizen of the world', like the 'Friend' of Churchill's poem.

132. Sir Fletcher Norton, Attorney-General. See *An Epistle to William Hogarth*, note to 75.

135-6. The Sirens were sea nymphs who charmed many to their deaths through the irresistible beauty of their song. For Lord Mansfield, see *The Ghost,* note to 4, 797-800.

137. 'SOPHS' are sophists; in ancient Greece, 'sophist' was used in a negative sense to describe anyone who gave intellectual training for money (and was thus an ignoble contrast with the idea of a philosopher). Churchill may also be playing on the more modern meaning of a sophist as a specious and false reasoner.

142-3. The reference is to Demosthenes, regarded as the greatest Athenian orator, and Marcus Tullius Cicero, the Roman equivalent.

179. As elsewhere, 'Science' refers to intellectual knowledge in general.

188. 'HOTTENTOT' (the name of a South African tribe) was a derogatory term used to indicate an uncivilised and ignorant person.

212. Churchill's two stock anti-Butean insults, Scotland and the Stuart

monarchy (one inherently associated by the other).
213-16. A veiled reference to Bute and the contemporary decline of England since the earlier 'freedoms won' by the so-called 'Glorious Revolution' and constitutional monarchy of 1688.
226. An allusion to the Sermon on the Mount (Matthew 7:16-20): 'Ye shall know them by their fruits'.
244. As elsewhere, 'Candour' means 'freedom from malice, favourable disposition, kindliness', rather than the slightly different 'honesty'.
245-58. The 'Friend's' argument is a traduction of Alexander Pope's *Essay on Man* (1733-4), a philosophical justification of the divinely ordained workings of the universe, which claims, amongst many other things, that man's perspective is necessarily finite, and thus unable to understand the universe as a whole (though this should be aspired towards). Churchill's veiled attack here on Pope's poem was one of many criticisms of what was seen as its facile and abstract optimism (see, most famously, Johnson, *Lives of The Poets*, 3, pp.243-4).
262. 'Ye cannot serve God and mammon' (Matthew 6:24).
303-4. Probably a reference to Wilkes's fleeing to France to avoid arrest, on 24 December 1763, after the disasters in the Lords and Commons and his duel with Martin.
319. Churchill is here possibly inverting Adam's warning in *Paradise Lost* about man's resistance to sin: 'Secure from outward force; within himself/ The danger lies, yet lies within his power:/ Against his will he can receive no harm' (Book 9, 348-50).
323. A reference to the Peace of the Treaty of Paris.
326-8. An allusion to the denial of Wilkes's parliamentary privilege, in his arrest in April 1763, and the double standard of voting *An Essay on Woman* a breach of the privilege of William Warburton in the House of Lords in November.
334. Here, 'reach' has the now obsolete sense of 'attain understanding of'.
392-99. This echoes follows Pope's *Epilogue to the Satires*, Dialogue II, 10-23, where Pope is asked to 'Spare then the Person' and (contradictorily) to 'name them'.

401-14. An allusion to Lord Chief Justice Mansfield, and his allowing the amending of the prosecution case before the trial of Wilkes *in absentia* in 1764. See *The Ghost,* note to 4:797-800, and the Introduction.

421-3. A reference to the recent acquittal of Philip Carteret Webb by the petty jury of Middlesex on 22 May 1764, in his trial for perjury before Lord Mansfield. Mansfield, Tooke reports (3, p.207), 'in his charge to the jury, on this occasion, too pointedly delivered his sentiments in favour of the defendant.' The case resulted from the action brought by Wilkes against Webb's colleague Robert Wood for illegal arrest. See *An Epistle to William Hogarth,* note to 200. Wilkes's trial for libel *in absentia* in February 1764 at the Court of King's Bench had also taken place under the care of Mansfield and a Middlesex jury. Mansfield had advised the jury to only find evidence of Wilkes's publication and printing of the *North Briton* No.45 (rather than have to prove the libel itself), hence, in part, Churchill's insinuation here.

432-9. The 'Grand Tour', the supposed introduction of young aristocrats to the traditions of European culture and civilisation. It was widely regarded as an opportunity for young men to indulge their vices away from Britain; Pope introduced a satire of a Grand Tourist into Book 4 of the *Dunciad* (1742), 293-334. See Jeremy Black, *The British and the Grand Tour* (London: Croom Helm, 1975), pp.109-24.

454-7. In India, a nabob was originally a provincial governor under the Mogul Emperors. As European influence grew, the word was applied more generally to the British returning from India with enhanced status or wealth (often carrying the insinuation of such wealth having being gathered nefariously). In this context, Churchill is referring to the rule of the British East India Company, which had instituted puppet native 'Nabobs' as rulers of Bengal; one of these, Mir Kassim, had been fomenting rebellion against the Company since 1763. The resulting rioting and intermittent warfare drew attention to the Company's political and economic hegemony in the area, the notorious abuses of this power for commercial gain, and the Company's general lack of accountability.

466. Churchill uses 'sterling' in the obsolete sense of 'having currency' – thus, he means 'if your observations prove to be true'.

473. The British East India Company.

474-9. The chaotic state of affairs in Bengal, and the internal conflict in the Company had been made public by a debate in the Court of Proprietors in London in March 1764, which ended with their asking Robert Clive, who had done more than anyone else in developing the rule of the Company in India, to return as Governor of Bengal and restore order.

482-4. Churchill is commenting on the trade monopoly, and on the absence of legislation which ensured that the Company could not be easily made answerable for its actions in India.

486-91. Clive had received a 'jaghire', a military rank with an annuity, from Mir Jaffir, then Nawab of Bengal, in 1759. It was worth some £28,000 annually. His right to receive this was the source of his argument with the Company Directors. Clive refused to accept the Governership of Bengal until a board of Directors more sympathetic to him had been elected (an election he helped to manipulate). After his right to the annuity for the next ten years was confirmed, he sailed to take up his appointment on 4 June 1764. See James P. Lawford, *Clive: Proconsul of India* (London: Allen & Unwin, 1976), pp.316-25, and Philip Lawson, *The East India Company: a Short History* (London: Longman, 1993), pp.92-6, 104-5. Churchill's parting shot suggests that more unwholesome secrets will be forthcoming from Clive's present and future conduct. From a relatively humble beginning, Clive had amassed an enormous amount of wealth from his Indian experiences, and charges of self-interest would surround him for the rest of his career, until a parliamentary enquiry of 1772-3 examined his conduct as Governor of Bengal.

The 'Dedication to the Sermons'

Text from first edition. Proofs of the poem given to Wilkes by Churchill are in the British Museum (C. 61. c.3); the one notable deviation is quoted below.

A volume of Churchill's sermons was published posthumously in February 1765, with the 'Dedication' attached. As the publication of such a devout volume was out of character (to say the least), it was assumed by Churchill's early biographers that Churchill sold the sermons for purely financial gain, and had no hand in them: it was speculated that they were compilations of earlier texts, or taken from the sermons of his father (See Brown, p.230, n.17; Grant, p.567, Tooke, 3, pp.313, 318-9) The 'Dedication' is thought to be an unfinished fragment of a planned larger work. In the first edition, a note signed by John Churchill reads 'It is presumed the sudden death of the Author will sufficiently apologise for the Dedication remaining unfinished'. However, Alan Fisher notes that 'The fragmentary appearance may be deceiving, because this poem seems to be the least actually fragmentary of Churchill's poems' ('The Stretching of Augustan Satire: Charles Churchill's Dedication to Warburton', *Journal of English and Germanic Philology* 72 (1973), pp.360-377, 360). The poem is perhaps the best example of Churchill's poetic development in his short career: its asides, enjambed statements and qualifications produce very subtle movements of tone in the poem's address. The result is ironic praise of its subject, William Warburton, that quickly insinuates itself as utter contempt, producing what Yvor Winters called 'a horrifying judgment of moral ugliness' (*Forms of Discovery* (Denver: Alan Swallow, 1962), p.145). The poem shows that Churchill's writing near his death was far from exhausted, particularly in its stylistic impetus.

1. William Warburton (1698-1779), Bishop of Gloucester since 1762. Warburton was the most ferocious literary and theological controversialist of a period that did not lack for rancorous dispute. Of his many quarrels, some of the most significant proceeded from his executorship and posthumous editing of the works of his friend Alexander Pope (1751), and his edition of Shakespeare (1747). His most important theological work was the extraordinary (and inevitably controversial) unfinished *Divine Legation of Moses* (1738-41, with many subsequent additions and enlargements). Warburton earned Churchill's dislike through his denunciation of Wilkes's *An Essay on Woman* in the House of Lords in November 1763; the 'notes' to Wilkes's ribald poem had been attributed to Warburton, probably in mockery of his notoriously verbose annotations in his editions of Pope and Shakespeare. Churchill's choice

of a 'Dedication' to Warburton was itself ironic: Warburton's dedications to his patrons in his works could be ingratiating even by the standards of the time, and the third edition of the second part of the *Divine Legation of Moses* (1757), contained a Dedication to Churchill's old enemy Lord Mansfield, one of Warburton's patrons. A comprehensive (though perhaps surprisingly sympathetic) account of Warburton's tempestuous career can be found in A. W. Evans, *Warburton and the Warburtonians: a Study in Some Eighteenth Century Controversies* (Oxford: Clarendon Press, 1932).

5. Churchill's mention of flattery is deliberate: Warburton's many enemies accused him of fawning around great men for advancement. His enemy Bolingbroke, in their quarrel over Pope's legacy, exclaimed that 'You have signalized yourself by affecting to be the bully of Mr P[ope]'s Memory, into whose Acquaintance, the latter End of the poor Man's Life, you was introduced by your nauseous flattery', Henry St John Bolingbroke, *A Familiar Epistle to the Most Impudent Man Living* (London, 1749), p.12.

7. '*Orthodox* Divine' is a reference to the reception of Warburton's *Divine Legation of Moses*: 'The novelty of the arguments in the Divine Legation, the paradoxical appearance of its data, and the variety of learning displayed in it, had excited the attention of the world, and many of the Orthodox Divines became alarmed at the idea of its being a covert attack on Christianity, instead of a defence of it.' John Nicholls, *Literary Anecdotes of the Eighteenth Century*, 9 vols. (London, 1812-16), V, p.549.

13. The 'note' is a reference to the prolixity of the annotation in Warburton's editions of Pope and Shakespeare. It also remarks upon Warburton's editorial addition to the notes of Pope's *Dunciad Variorum* in 1751 in order to discredit Thomas Edwards, a lawyer who had satirised the excesses and pomposity of his Shakespeare edition in his *Canons of Criticism* (1748). (See *The Dunciad*, Book 4, 567-8, in *The Works of Alexander Pope*, ed. William Warburton, 9 vols. (1751), 5, p.309, for Warburton's additional note, which is also criticised by Churchill in *The Duellist*, 753-64).

16-21. A possible allusion to the benefits that Warburton has gathered from being Pope's executor, and from his closeness to Ralph Allen (see 27-8).

25-6. Wilkes's annotation of these lines suggests that it is a reference to the attempted bribing into silence of Churchill by Lord Holland, after the advertisement for his poem 'Ayliffe's Ghost' had appeared. See *An Epistle to William Hogarth,* note to 140.

27-8. Ralph Allen (1694-1764), made a fortune out of reforming the postage system; well-known as a philanthropist, he was a friend of many writers, including Alexander Pope, Samuel Richardson and Henry Fielding (who modelled the character of Squire Allworthy in *Tom Jones* on him). Warburton married Allen's niece, Gertrude Tucker, in 1746, and had inherited Allen's not inconsiderable fortune at the time of Churchill's writing (he would inherit Allen's estate at Prior Park two years later).

It is possible that the reference to 'offspring' and an 'heir' is meant to remind Warburton of the rumour that his son was not his own, but the result of his wife's alleged affair with Thomas Potter (1718-59), dissolute son of the Archbishop of Canterbury, Wilkes's friend and probably the co-author of *An Essay on Woman*; if so, this gives the lines a very different meaning. See Don Nichol, 'Slander, Scandal and Satire' (*TLS*, 28 January 2000, p.14), for more details of the rumours of Potter's affair with Warburton's wife. Walpole had described the absurdity of Warburton's conduct when damning Wilkes and *An Essay on Woman* in the House of Lords as 'heightened by its being known that Potter, his wife's gallant, had had the chief hand in the verses' (Walpole, 1, p.248).

36. Warburton's 'Mitre' is a metonym for his Bishopric.

42. As in An *Epistle to William Hogarth*, 115, 'Lawn sleeves' (lawn being the linen used for the sleeves of a bishop) is a metonym for the office of a bishop.

44. In *Romeo and Juliet*, Lady Capulet (describing the Count Paris) claims that "tis much pride/ For fair without the fair within to hide' (Iiii, 91-92).

46. 'Complacency' is here used in a sense now obsolete, meaning 'disposition to please others', a heavily ironic usage, in the context of Churchill's poem.

49-50. As Churchill suggests, Warburton was not renowned for his good looks.

55-59. 'The Warburtons were an old Cheshire family who traced their descent from one of William the Conqueror's companions' (Evans, *Warburton*, p.3). Warburton's father died when he was only eight years old, which may explain 'Sire unknown'.

60. As an appendix to his *Dissertation on Ecclesiastical Antiquity* (1751), Warburton's friend John Jortin printed an account (written for him by Warburton) of the prophecies of Arise Evans, seventeenth century Welsh author of *An Eccho from Heaven*, which predicted 'that four Stuarts should reign in England after Cromwell' (Evans, *Warburton*, p.190). Despite his obvious lack of belief in Evans's predictions, Warburton's contribution 'afterwards subjected him to much ridicule' (Nicholls, *Literary Anecdotes*, 5, p.603).

73-81. A reference to Churchill's life in the church, and his curacy of the parish of St John the Evangelist, Westminster from 1758-63, where he followed his father.

76. According to Brown (p.25), the rector of St John the Evangelist, Joseph Sims, 'appears to have devoted his attention principally to his other parish in East Ham.'

77-8. In the proof sheets given to Wilkes by Churchill, the following couplet appeared at this point, before being crossed out by Wilkes:

> Whiche accents of rebuke could nevr bear,
> Nor would have heeded Christ, had Christ been there;

87. See Proverbs, 4.12 and 16.9 for variants on this theme; Churchill adopts a general language of religious sentiment in describing his ironic ideal of Warburton's devotion.

93. Job's comforter Elihu remarks on his having heretically said that 'It profiteth a man nothing that he should delight himself with God' (Job, 34:9).

94-6. In referring to Warburton's self-aggrandising editing of Pope and Shakespeare, Churchill is drawing on Pope's satirising of the editing of Richard Bentley. See the *Epistle to Dr Arburthnot*, 157-72 and *The Dunciad* (1743), 4, 210-15.

111. The reference to 'adopted son' is another cruel reminder of his wife's alleged affair with Thomas Potter. See note to 27-8.

131-3. A reference to the denunciation of *An Essay on Woman* in the

House of Lords.

133-9. In the Lords, Warburton supposedly 'foamed with the violence of a Saint Dominic; vaunted that he had combated infidelity, and laid it under his feet; and said, the blackest fiends in hell would not keep company with Wilkes, and then begged Satan's pardon for comparing them together' (Walpole, 1, p.247).

140. For Thomas Potter, see note to 27-8.

151.Warburton had started a career as a lawyer (his family profession) but changed to the Church, motivated apparently by intellectual interests. It is also possible that he was offered good ecclesiastical livings by his early patron, Sir Robert Sutton (see Evans, *Warburton*, pp.8-9).

152. St Paul reports that Demas has forsaken him, and the faith (2 Timothy 4:10).

158-60. See note to 151. It suits Churchill's purpose to show Warburton's move to the Church as further evidence of his mendacity and bad faith. Warburton's enemies often reminded him of his past as an attorney (see Evans, *Warburton*, p.12).

162. Warburton's patron Lord Mansfield. See note to *The Ghost*, 4, 1797-1800. End. Cetera Desunt – 'the rest is lacking'. Presumed to have been inserted by Churchill's brother John, who saw the volume of sermons through the press.

Index of Titles and First Lines

AMONGST the sons of men how few are known	32
Dark was the Night, by Fate decreed	53
The 'Dedication to the Sermons'	82
[From *The Duellist*]	53
An Epistle to William Hogarth	32
FAR off (no matter whether East or West,	57
The Farewell	65
FAREWELL to Europe, and at once, farewell	65
FREEDOM came next, but scarce was seen,	5
[From *The Ghost*]	4
[From *Gotham*]	57
HEALTH to great GLOSTER–from a man unknown,	82
Horrid, *unwieldy, without Form*,	4
Last GARRICK came,–Behind him throng a train	1
The Prophecy of Famine: a Scots Pastoral	13
[From *The Rosciad*]	1
When CUPID first instructs his darts to fly	13